The Soul Collector

By

Joni Mayhan

Also by Joni Mayhan

on Amazon.com for Kindle and Paperback

Lightning Strikes (Angels of Ember trilogy – Book 1)

Ember Rain (Angels of Ember trilogy – Book 2)

Angel Storm (Angels of Ember trilogy – Book 3)

Bones in the Basement – Surviving the S.K. Pierce Haunted Victorian Mansion (true paranormal story)

Ghostly Defences – A Sensitive's Guide for Protection

Acknowledgments

I can honestly say that I wouldn't have survived this if it weren't for some truly wonderful friends. I think you learn the meaning of true friendship when you are in a place where you need help, but have nothing to give in return except gratitude. They stuck beside me, even though the mere thought of being around me was terrifying for most of them. The Soul Collector could have easily latched onto any one of them as well.

Thank you, Sandy MacLeod, for always being there for me. We've been through some pretty terrifying times together, as well as some hysterical ones.

This story would have ended much differently if it weren't for Michael Cram, Stephen Flaherty, and Nancy Cram. I am so blessed to have you in my life. Thank you for dropping everything to help me. I'll never forget it.

Appreciation also to Tina Aube, for giving me a safe place to retreat to, and for staying with me, even when every cell in your body told you to flee.

I am also eternally grateful to the coven of witches in Maine. You ladies truly turned things around for me.

I am also thankful to my children, Laura and Trevor, and to my family for always keeping me in their thoughts. Your love kept me buoyant when I started sinking.

Thank you to my proof readers: Aprille Bernard, Jo Ann Dinsmore, Alex Zacceo, Madison Plante, and Barb Wright for your expertise. Many thanks also go to Michael Robishaw for reviewing my protection list, and helping me during the writing of this book.

I appreciate the following people for allowing me to use your photos: Keith Glenn, Jimmy Bennett, Derek Cormier, and Chris Cox. You were part of my journey, whether you realized it or not.

Lastly, even though I didn't mention her by name, I am very thankful to the psychic medium who helped me I hope you find the happiness you long for.

Love and light to you all.

For my friends, who offered me a life raft in a drowning sea.

Sandy MacLeod

Tina Aube

Michael Cram

Stephen Flaherty

Nancy Cram

Chapter 1

I was warned to never talk about him.

I was supposed to just walk away and forget the entire experience, totally erasing him from my memory. If I didn't, there was a very good chance he could come back to find me again. I held onto this story for several years, trying to follow their advice, but I just couldn't.

I needed to tell my story.

I wasn't in a very good place when he found me. I was at the end of a two-year relationship with someone I thought I would spend the rest of my life with, growing old together. When he walked away so suddenly, it left my whole life in shambles.

With my entire family living a thousand miles away, I didn't have anyone to turn to. I'm not the kind of person who cries to other people about her problems. I swallowed the pain whole, and then allowed it to consume me. It burrowed and spread, reaching into every cell of my being, leaving me nothing more than a shell.

I was forty-seven years old, living in a small house in the rural town of Barre, Massachusetts. I purchased the nine-hundred square foot ranch house after my divorce in 2005, hoping to find a place to rest before moving onto my happily-ever-after. Six years later, I was in the same place with no hope in sight.

After spending weeks locked inside my house with the curtains drawn, I finally decided to get out and do something. People told me that staying busy was the best cure for a broken heart, so I tried.

A friend invited me to go ghost hunting. As it turns out, it was the worst thing I could have done. It brought me to the Soul Collector.

(Below: Joni investigating in the basement of one of her favorite haunted locations.

Chapter 2

I got into ghost hunting quite by accident.

I spent a solid three years after my divorce hiding out in my house. I didn't have any friends to speak of and had nowhere to go. Besides, people were hurtful and scary. I preferred spending the time with my pets or by myself, writing, reading, and watching movies.

Sometimes I feel like a hopeless cause. I've never been socially adept. Since grade school, I've had a difficult time interacting with my peers. Being small as a child, I was often picked on by schoolyard bullies. I didn't fare much better in high school. It seemed like every time I allowed myself to get close to someone, I ended up getting hurt. In the end, I decided it was better to just be alone and save myself the pain. It turned out to be a lonely decision that I would soon reconsider.

The one friend I retained into adulthood was actually an old high-school boyfriend who still lived in Indiana. Finding ourselves both single after years of marriage, we forged a long-distance friendship. John was the one who got me to come out of my shell. First, he talked me into setting up an online dating profile.

Initially, I was almost giddy with all the attention I was suddenly getting. After going for days without seeing another soul, I was being invited out onto dates with eligible men. John was doing the same thing back in Indiana and we started using one another as sounding boards.

"I need a woman's point of view," he'd say, then ask me a question. I'd offer my best advice, eventually helping him connect with his soon-to-be wife Melinda. I'd run situations and concerns past him for a man's point of view. We spent many long nights on the phone just chatting and helping each other through the hard times.

"You need to get out of your house," he told me one day. "Why don't you look into Meetup.com? Find something you like on there." He'd found a kayaking group there and enjoyed the occasional weekend outing with a group of people who shared his love of the water. He suggested I look into it to see if I could find a ghost hunting group, knowing how much I was into the paranormal.

While I had never investigated before, I was well versed on the subject. I'd spent the past few years amassing quite a collection of books on the paranormal. I read them from cover to cover, over and over again. I understood the difference between a residual haunting and an intelligent spirit. I was intrigued by the concept of EVPs, and even had my own digital recorder to record spirit voices. It was time to put my knowledge to work.

I took John's advice and quickly found a paranormal meet-up group. I signed up for their next event and waited eagerly for the day to arrive.

The first event was a wash out. The people who ran the event were a flaky bunch. They set up a meet-up at the Hoosic Tunnel in North Adams, Massachusetts.

Spanning over five miles, the tunnel snakes through the base of the Berkshire Mountains, cutting a path that was paved by bloodshed and death. People who dared enter it sometimes found themselves in the company of ghosts. Other people were smart enough not to walk several miles into a tunnel where an active train tunnel runs.

I had no doubt that the tunnel contained residual energy. The ground and stone have a tendency to absorb the vibrations from traumatic events in the past, replaying them like a movie, over and over again. A good example of this is Gettysburg. You can't walk out onto a battlefield without feeling the hair on the back of your neck prickle. It's as though Mother Earth is telling you, "Something happened here." People often see soldiers, or hear cannon fire, as history replays itself, but they seldom make contact with the apparitions.

While residual hauntings were interesting, making contact with an intelligent spirit was my overall goal. I had high hopes for the Hoosic Tunnel.

I brought my twenty-year-old daughter, Laura, with me to the event. We were both appropriately nervous about venturing inside. As we walked down the tracks leading to the tunnel, I could feel the anticipation rapidly turn to anxiety.

"What if a train comes?" I asked my daughter, eyeing the narrow space between the tracks and the stone walls. We might be able to press ourselves against the sides and hope for the best, but it sounded horrifically dangerous.

Laura shrugged. Suddenly, it didn't seem like such a great idea.

Several members of the meet-up group were gathered near the tunnel entrance. As we approached them, we could feel the air grow colder by several degrees.

"I'm glad to see you brought jackets," an older woman said to us. "It's quite a bit colder inside the tunnel," she said.

After quick introductions, we learned that she was the meet-up leader.

Something about her truly gave me the creeps. I wasn't sure if it was the way she looked, with her mop of unbrushed hair, or the way she was dressed in layers of skirts and shawls, accessorized by thick sandals with socks. It may have just been the wild look in her eyes that made me think of an escaped mental patient. Either way, she made me uncomfortable.

She had two other investigators with her. One was a younger woman who was the equipment expert. She walked around with an EMF meter in her hand. The other was a tall, thin man, who just stood back and watched.

"Are you getting anything?" I asked the younger woman.

"No. Nothing so far," she told me, showing me her EMF meter.

My daughter gave me a curious look, so I explained what an EMF meter does.

"It measures changes in the electro-magnetic field in an area. If a ghost comes close to us, we might see a spike in the reading," I told her. While I was anxious to have a paranormal experience, I hoped it would be a little more substantial than a blip on someone's meter.

I took my digital recorder out of my pocket and started recording, hoping for an EVP. I showed it to my daughter.

"When a ghost speaks to us, we usually can't hear them. But, if you are recording it with a digital recorder, you might record their response. It's called an EVP: electronic voice phenomena."

I asked a few questions, and then listened to the audio, hearing nothing but silence. I was disappointed, but was still hopeful. If we tried it again inside the tunnel, we might have better results.

We lingered near the entrance for several minutes. The others were milling around, talking. I was ready to go inside and get started. "Are we going in?" I finally asked.

The leader turned to look at me, her face frozen with fright. "No. I can't go in there. This place is sheer evil," she said, hopefully not noticing when I rolled my eyes.

"So, what are we going to do?" I asked, growing appropriately agitated. We paid ten dollars apiece for the experience, but we weren't going in?

"You can go in, if you want to," the leader said. "But, I'm

staying right here." Her team members stuck to her side, refusing to budge as well.

I sighed and looked around, wondering what to do. It was a beautiful blue-sky day in early May. The leaves were just popping out on the trees, and the air was filled with the sweet scent of spring. We'd driven nearly two hours to be there. It seemed a shame to waste the trip only to just turn around and leave.

I turned to my daughter. "Wanna go in a little ways?" I asked.

"Might as well," she said, without much enthusiasm.

We'd spent thirteen years living in a haunted house. While we were both curious about the paranormal, we were both a little apprehensive. Sometimes opening a door to something brings you closer than you anticipated.

I'd read that ghosts often drained the batteries on your equipment, so I was well prepared for the walk. I'd put fresh batteries into four flashlights. I gave two to my daughter and kept the other two for myself. There was no way I was going to be submerged in the darkness with no light. It just wasn't going to happen.

As we were getting ready to walk in, three men joined us at the mouth of the tunnel. The oldest man was obviously the father of one of the younger men. They wanted to check out the tunnel but didn't have a flashlight. Not really thinking, I offered to let them follow us.

I should preface this with the fact that I am a little too trusting of others, at least at first. Sometimes my common sense takes a backseat to my willingness to please. It's a fault I will find myself making over and over in my life.

I walked in first, with my daughter behind me, and the three men trailing along behind us.

The tunnel was eerie. The minute we walked inside, the

darkness quickly enveloped us with cold, damp fingers. I shined my light around, trying to get a feel for the place.

The tall, curved ceilings were lined with bricks. Many of the bricks had fallen, which was evident from the broken shards at our feet. Graffiti graced nearly every wall like strange artwork.

The tracks were difficult to walk on and water dripped from the ceilings, creating echoes through the tunnel. After walking for ten minutes, we were deep in the heart of the mountain. I turned around, surprised to find the tunnel opening no more than a tiny circle, floating in the darkness behind us.

It suddenly occurred to me what I was doing. I willingly led my beautiful daughter into a dark tunnel with three men I didn't know. While they seemed normal, I had no idea of their intent. My active imagination went into overdrive. What if they were bad men? I didn't think that serial killers usually hunted in packs, but who really knew?

"Ummm....you guys aren't serial killers," I said, trying to make it sound like a joke.

There was a long silence before one of the men finally spoke.

"I guess it's a little late to be asking that question, isn't it?" one of them said. He had a smile in his voice when he said it, but my discomfort level was already rising into the red zone.

"Let's turn around," I suggested, praying they wouldn't take that moment to reveal some evil personalities.

Forgetting all about my desire to do another EVP session, we turned around and made our way out of the tunnel in record time. Thankfully, the men were nothing more than true gentlemen and we parted ways at the mouth of the tunnel. I just stood there as they walked back towards the parking lot, feeling very foolish.

"What a stupid thing to do," I whispered to my daughter. I

was so angry with myself for putting her in possible danger. If a train didn't run us over, the strangers could have turned out to be something other than just nice, ordinary men. What kind of mother was I?

I didn't have long to berate myself, because the meet-up leader was quickly approaching.

"Did you feel anything?" she asked, wide-eyed.

I was embarrassed she was even asking me. Admitting that I *did* or *didn't* feel something felt like social suicide. What if someone heard us? They'd think I was just as crazy as she was.

Honestly, the only thing I felt was the sense of intrigue followed by the rush of overwhelming fear. I wasn't afraid of ghosts. I was afraid of the men walking behind us and the situation I'd put us in. We nearly ran back to the car.

It would be several years later before I'd try it again.

(Below) Joni's daughter Laura, at the Hoosic Tunnel

Chapter 3

I was understandably apprehensive when I got another notification from the meet-up group. Our last event turned out to be less than expected. I wasn't sure I wanted to put myself through that again.

All I wanted was a true paranormal experience. I wanted to go on a real investigation, complete with all the tools of the trade. I wanted to play with an EMF detector, and then watch the numbers rise as a spirit approached. I longed to take part in an actual EVP session, listening to my recorded audio later, hearing the whispered voices of the dead. Mostly though, I wanted answers to my life-long questions of ghosts.

I think that everyone who gets into the field of paranormal investigating does so out of curiosity. There's just so much we don't know about the world around us. We walk through our world expecting everything to always be normal and sane, but sometimes we run into things that make us stop and think. I'd had my fair share of these moments and I wanted some of my questions answered.

I took a deep breath and signed up for the event, hoping it would end up different than my first ghost hunting experience.

I was relieved to discover that the crazy meet-up lady had left the group and was replaced by someone quite normal. Her name was Sandy MacLeod.

We were to meet in a town called Clinton, at the site of an old abandoned train tunnel.

Great, another tunnel.

I almost didn't go, but my curiosity won out in the end.

By this time, I was dating my now ex-boyfriend. While he

wasn't a believer in anything supernatural, he agreed to go with me and share the experience. I was happy to have him with me. Going to something like this alone truly scared me. I had no idea what to expect.

We met Sandy in a nearby parking lot and exchanged pleasantries. She was nothing like I expected. She was a middle-aged woman with fiery red hair and glasses. Her demeanor was very calm and patient as she carefully explained what we would be doing. She looked more like a teacher than a ghost hunter. I was immediately intrigued by her.

"She seems normal," I whispered to my boyfriend.

We followed her to a roadside parking area, and then climbed up a weedy hill to a path that led to the tunnel. It was very dark that night. The moon hid behind a bank of clouds, setting the mood for the evening. Sandy gathered us in a circle and began talking about protection.

"While it's unlikely anything will follow any of us home, it doesn't hurt to take precautions," she told us. She went through a list of ways to protect ourselves, ranging from reciting prayers to cleansing the air with sage. She went on to tell us that some people carried protective medals or stones in their pockets. Others called on spirit guides or guardian angels to keep them protected.

I rolled my eyes at the mention of spirit guides. I'd heard the term before, but lumped it in with all the other mystical creatures, like unicorns and dragons. *Here we go*, I thought to myself.

"Protection also involves safety," she went on to tell us. "We never go off anywhere alone. We always go in groups."

"Even to the bathroom?" someone asked, making the group giggle.

"Well, they don't have to go in with you, but you should at

least go to the area together," she said with a smile in her voice. She went onto to explain that being alone could be dangerous while investigating.

"What if one of you fell and got hurt? Or, what if you experienced something? You'd want someone there to witness it."

She sprayed us with an herbal spray that smelled faintly like pine trees and lavender, and then explained that it was a protection spray she purchased at a paranormal trade show. I just soaked it all in. I had so much to learn and was eager to get going.

We continued down the path, seeing the first hint of the tunnel emerging from the darkness. The excitement rose up in me like a small child on Christmas. I was finally going on a real ghost hunt! I couldn't have been happier.

Sandy handed out equipment for us to use, explaining each piece before turning us loose. We walked in groups, measuring the electromagnetic energy with detectors that would light up if there was a spike in energy. We walked up and down the quarter-mile train tunnel, finding very little.

Like in the Hoosic tunnel, water dripped from the ceilings and the walls were covered with graffiti. Discarded slivers of liquor bottles were mixed in with the chunky gravel, making it difficult to navigate. I stopped and looked around a few times, wondering about the whole concept of the paranormal.

Despite my experience with the first meet-up group, I was a firm believer in ghosts. I'd had a few experiences in my life that I couldn't explain. In some ways, I hoped that by getting closer to the subject, I might gain more insight to the things that had happened to me.

I had a lot of questions.

Seven other people attended, all having various levels of

experience. Some of them brought their own equipment, and others, like us, came with nothing more than flashlights and digital recorders. We didn't find anything overly exciting. No one shouted for us to "GET OUT" while we were there, and our meters only flickered a few times. Still though, it was the most fun I'd had in years. I was hooked.

As we were leaving, we mentioned to Sandy that we were going to Waverly Hills Sanatorium in Louisville, Kentucky, the next month. My sister, knowing how much I loved the paranormal, had booked a ghost hunt for my annual pilgrimage back home to Indiana. Sandy was excited to learn this.

"Do you mind if I come with you?" she asked.

I was elated. A real-life ghost hunter was coming with us! I couldn't wait to get home and call my sister, Leah. Instead of wandering around an abandoned Tuberculosis Hospital with no idea what we were doing, we were going with an experienced paranormal investigator.

It would be the beginning of a friendship that would prove very beneficial for both of us.

Chapter 4

Waverly Hills Sanatorium is a very eerie old building constructed in the early nineteen hundreds to house and care for patients suffering from tuberculosis. At the height of the disease, the sanatorium housed up to 150 patients at one time, many of them eventually succumbing to their illness. After the discovery of the antibiotic drug streptomycin, the hospital was closed. It would reopen in 1962, functioning for the next twenty years as a nursing home. In 1982 it closed its doors once more after reports of under-staffing and poor conditions made the news.

Reports of the hauntings there were legendary. Supposedly, over sixty-three thousand people died there over its seventy-one year history as a TB hospital and nursing home. Tuberculosis deaths were so high at one point, the hospital built a tunnel leading to the bottom of the hill where the recently deceased could be removed without distressing the remaining patients.

We followed a long, tree-lined lane, anticipation nearly overwhelming us. When we rounded the corner and the building came into view, I gasped at the sight of it. It was huge!

My sister's husband had invited some of his friends from work to join us. They were a rowdy group, prone to making ghost sounds and laughing at nearly everything. I quickly suggested that we break up into two groups.

A young high-spirited woman took us on an hour-long tour, telling us stories that made the hair on the back of my neck stand up. We walked down the dark corridors, getting brief glimpses of the rooms leading off of them. We'd see flashes of barren rooms with ivy growing through the windows as we walked, hoping to catch a glimpse of something paranormal.

She took us to the fifth floor where a nurse supposedly

committed suicide after learning she was pregnant. The stories surrounding her death were varied. Some said she was impregnated by a doctor from the hospital, who refused to help her after she became pregnant. Others said she had been raped, and couldn't get past the traumatic event. Either way, her spirit had remained at the hospital. Investigators often reported sightings of her, lingering in the doorway.

Then, the guide took us onto the veranda, where patients were provided with "fresh air" treatment, thought to help tuberculosis patients. As I stood there, looking out at the dark landscape, it wasn't difficult to imagine the spirits of the dead. I could feel them, hanging back, watching us, probably wondering what we were doing. It made me wonder why someone would choose to stay here. If I were a ghost, a hospital would be the last place I'd haunt. If given a choice, I'd haunt the beaches of Tahiti.

The history tour was fascinating. I felt like I'd stepped back in time and was getting to witness something most people would never get the chance to see.

The abandoned hospital had sat empty for many decades, which was evident from the deteriorating conditions of the rooms. Aging fixtures still adorned the pealing ceilings, and the walls were chipped and faded. It wasn't hard to imagine the hospital bustling with activity, the empty spaces filled with beds and ailing patients. I didn't get overly nervous until she took us to the fourth floor, where she told us a story that would haunt us for the rest of the night.

She told us about the creeper.

She said that an unknown entity was often seen on the fourth floor. The first time she saw it, she fled the hospital, swearing she'd never return. She said that while it looked like a human, with arms and legs and a head, it crawled across the ceilings in a crouched position before dropping down to the floor in front of surprised witnesses.

I spent the rest of the night staring at the ceiling.

It made me wonder about this strange paranormal world. I'd read about ghosts hanging around old buildings, and had even learned about demons, but creepers? That was something I was truly unprepared for. The thought of an entity crawling across the ceiling woke up my imagination. If there were creepers, what else was there?

The investigation was appropriately chilling. The hallways were long and dark. Sounds could be heard in the distance. Shadows moved across the walls and ceilings. My boyfriend even saw his first full-body apparition. The figure of a man moved silently past him in the darkness, instantly transforming him into a believer.

(Below) Joni at Waverly Hills Sanatorium

I learned a great deal about the paranormal world that night, finally experiencing things I'd only read about or watched on television. Later, I listened to the audio I recorded on my digital voice recorder, thrilled to have captured my first series of EVPs. We returned home with the promise to meet up with Sandy again soon.

Sandy and I became instant friends after that event, something that had only happened to me a handful of times in my entire life. We began getting together on a regular basis, checking out cemeteries and abandoned ruins, then comparing notes on the evidence we captured. It was at this time when I truly started paying closer attention to the ringing in my ears.

I'd turn my head back and forth, trying to pinpoint the location of the ring. Unlike normal tinnitus, I could actually hear the sound getting louder as I got closer to the entity. Over time, I began to realize that the tones I was hearing were all different. Female spirits had a very high, crystalline tone, while males sounded more like static.

Sandy helped me through this, amazed at my ability, until she started developing one of her own. She discovered that her head tingled on one side at the same time my ears were ringing. Like amateur scientists, we began testing our abilities, amazed to find that we often started getting spirit responses on our recorders when we both felt a presence nearby.

We were elated. We began investigating in earnest, and sought out paranormal psychic mediums to verify our claims. Most of the mediums we met were surprised we were just now learning about our abilities.

"You have far more ability than what you're using," one psychic medium told me.

The thought was distressing, but alluring all the same. I

wasn't sure how I felt about it and I certainly wasn't going to tell anyone about it. They'd think I was blue-goose crazy.

As it would turn out, these humble paranormal beginnings would soon lead me on a terrifying adventure I'd never forget. I'm just thankful I had Sandy with me for it.

I couldn't have survived it without her.

(Below) Joni and Sandy in Salem 2012

Chapter 5

By the fall of 2011, I'd investigated at dozens of locations, and progressed from participating in a meet-up group to joining an actual ghost hunting team. After six months on the team, I suddenly found myself in the role of Massachusetts's Director, after the former director stepped down.

Knowing I lacked the experience, I made sure I surrounded myself with people who had investigated for years. Sandy was my assistant director, something she took very seriously. At one point, our Massachusetts team had thirty-five members, making our team the largest in the national group.

As we started out, we pretty much stuck to local events, checking out places we'd seen on paranormal television shows, while trying to find answers for all those questions about the unknown. We checked out Rolling Hills Asylum in Bethany, New York; the Houghton Mansion in North Adams, Massachusetts; and the Haunted Victorian Mansion in Gardner, Massachusetts, just to name a few. By the time I ran into the Soul Collector, I had amassed just enough knowledge to become a danger to myself.

By this time, I'd already developed a true knack for getting EVPs, Electronic Voice Phenomena. When I turned on my digital voice recorder and asked questions during an investigation, the spirits spoke to me. I didn't understand why they singled me out, giving very clear responses to my questions while they ignored others, but I was just happy to be successful at something. My entire life up to that point felt like a near miss.

I'd spent twenty years trying to find my way as a writer, only to be shot down by countless agents and publishing houses. I tried to open my own pet store in the early eighties, but was stopped short due to financing issues. I was married for nearly twenty years, but found myself divorced and all alone at an age when most women were comfortably settled into their lives. I needed something to cling to, something I could claim as my own. So I dove deeply into ghost hunting, something that would end up being my eventual undoing.

In the beginning, it was just pure entertainment. I was invited to explore creepy places, where I had the opportunity to speak with actual dead people. As I gained more confidence, I became fearless. I would be the first person who dared to go into the darkest, scariest places. I'd crawl into basements, sit by myself in a totally dark room, and invite the spirits to communicate with me. It was an adrenaline rush, a way to push my life to the edge, a way to feel something other than misery. And, I became good at it.

I booked investigations at the creepiest locations I could find. Sometimes I had two ghost hunts in one weekend. I was completely captivated.

Imagine, actually speaking to the dead.

The spirit world fascinated me. I wanted to learn more.

I asked questions I'd always wanted to know the answers to, and I began getting very clear responses. They told me that Heaven was beautiful, that they were lonely and enjoyed talking with us. They told me their ages, the places where they lived, and the reasons why they still clung to the living world.

I began to develop a sensitivity to spirits. I learned that the ear ringing I'd lived with all my life was more than just tinnitus. I could actually track them around the room, knowing immediately where they were by the volume of the tone I was hearing. I soon learned there was an actual name for this. I was clairaudient.

Most people who are clairaudient hear actual voices, but my case was different. I wasn't sure if I was picking up on the vibration they made, or if it was something more internal. All I knew what that could hear them.

The tones moved in, almost swooping down upon me. Some tones were high, while others were low. As they move further away, the tone grows softer. Once I started working with it, it grew stronger.

At first, it was like having a new toy. I no longer needed an EMF meter to know if a spirit was with us. I could feel them drift into the room, my ears ringing with a tone that would allow me to know if they were male or female. I found that if I listened to the tone, I could literally pull them in closer. It was like a "here kitty-kitty" for the spirit world.

And they spoke to me on my digital recorder. I didn't understand why all this was happening to me until I came far too close to one.

After the break up with my boyfriend, I really didn't want to do anything. I lost my luster for ghost hunting. I just wanted to spend long hours on the sofa watching an endless array of mindless television shows.

When Sandy called me to remind me of our upcoming weekend investigation to the Rose Island Lighthouse, I wasn't even sure I wanted to go. It would be a bittersweet trip for me. I had purchased two tickets, but would end up going alone.

As the boat slipped through the water and the island came into view, my mood lifted substantially. The island was beautiful. It was just what I needed.

The Rose Island Lighthouse sits on a small island just off the coast of Newport, Rhode Island. It was used during both World Wars as a Navy Torpedo Station, where explosives were stored. Built in 1870; it served as a functioning lighthouse until 1970, when the Newport Bridge was built nearby.

People had been reporting strange occurrences there for a long time. It was said that one of the lighthouse keepers hadn't left the island, nor had several others, including a young child. We were eager to check it out.

(Below) Rose Island Lighthouse

(Below) The Barracks

Thirty other team members signed up for the event, but we had the entire island to ourselves for the night. Windswept beaches led to grassy areas, where seagulls flocked by the dozens. The ocean breeze cleared my mind, while the constant wash of waves hitting the shore soothed my soul. The investigation wouldn't start until the evening, so I spent some quiet time just walking along the beach, picking up sea-glass.

By the time evening came, everyone was aptly excited. Cameras were placed in the reported hot spots, and batteries were replaced in equipment. We divided into five teams and planned out the night.

Contamination is the one thing we all tried to avoid. If we were running our digital recorders, trying to speak with the dead, the last thing we wanted was to have voices in the background. We'd have to review everything very carefully, making sure the spirit voices we heard were actually spirits and not another group passing by. By dividing up on the island, we cut down on the chances of ruining a session.

The investigation itself was interesting, but I wasn't really into it. I walked around with the group, exploring the buildings, listening to their excitement build with the opening of every closed door. We did a few EVP sessions in the lighthouse, but we weren't getting any readings on our equipment. My ears hadn't been ringing either, a clear sign a spirit or ghost was not present. We'd soon find out that the real action was at the barracks.

During the Revolutionary War, the island was used by both the British and the Americans to defend the nearby city of Newport. The long building, which served as sleeping quarters, sat off to the side of the lighthouse.

During an epidemic, the last room in the barracks was used as a quarantine shelter. Soldiers were carried there, sick with a disease that would eventually take their lives. How many men had died there? We had no idea. We just knew the minute we walked into the building we weren't alone.

I really wasn't in the mood to investigate. I just wanted something that would occupy my mind, and prevent me from having a pity party. I was quiet and just keep my thoughts to myself. This quickly changed when the activity began.

We walked into the first room of the barracks, at the very end of the long, narrow building. Three-foot thick windowsills flanked either side of the room, equipped with heavy wooden shutters that were pulled tight to keep out the elements. Since there were only a few chairs, I pulled myself up onto one of the windowsills for the EVP session.

We always try to remain as quiet as possible during EVP sessions. A scrape of a foot or a gurgle of a stomach will often sound like a spirit voice after it's recorded. Sitting still is usually the best option. If someone's stomach gurgled, we were careful to mark it on the recorder, so we would know later what it was. A really deep stomach growl could sound like a demon bellowing, so it's always a good idea to distinguish between the two.

As soon as I pulled myself up onto the windowsill, the shutter started bouncing inward, hitting me in the back. I figured it was just the wind, so after a few times of being startled by the sudden movement, I decided to switch windowsills and move to the other side of the room. I would later learn that I captured an EVP.

"Go back," a male voice said very clearly.

https://soundcloud.com/jonimayhan/barracks-room-7-go-back-after (EVP available on Soundcloud.com/jonimayhan)

Who was this? Was it a soldier who died in the room a hundred years earlier? Why did he choose to stay here?

I'd never learn the answers to these questions.

We ended the investigation by sleeping in the keeper's quarters. I had a room all to myself with a beautiful view of the Atlantic Ocean. The seagulls serenaded me all night long, sending their sad, lonely cries across the water. I snuggled up in the patchwork quilt, trying not to think about all of the reasons why I was alone.

I awoke the next morning, feeling much better about my life. The sun shone bright in a perfect blue sky, and the air smelled like salt and sand. It was hard to stay depressed in such a setting.

I sought out our team's psychic medium to see what she

thought of the island.

The night before, we had split up into separate groups to cut down on the contamination. We'd bumped into one another as we were moving around the island, but I had hadn't had a chance to really talk with her. I always enjoyed hearing about her experiences.

She could hone in on the entities, telling us more about them, filling in the blanks we could only guess about. Without her, we were at the mercy of our equipment, which wasn't always useful. Even though we prided ourselves as being a scientific based team, relying on documented proof instead of personal experiences, I loved learning what the psychic medium could tell us. She could literally lift the veil and see what was on the other side, something I found fascinating.

I had my mouth open to ask her about her night, but the concerned expression on her face stopped me short.

She pulled me aside.

"Do you know how many friends you have with you?" she asked me.

Since I'd begun working on my psychic abilities, I had started picking up paranormal hitchhikers, spirits who followed me, possibly thinking I could help them. At first it truly frightened me. I could hear them swirling around my head and tried to push them off as best as I could. Eventually, I just tried to live with it. There didn't seem to be any other option for me.

I knew I had at least one or two, because I could hear the tones around me.

"I'd say five," she told me. She then told me to practice a visualization. "See them in your mind getting on a boat. Now send that boat off to sea," she told me.

I tried. Honestly, I did. I closed my eyes and really cemented the image in my mind, but when I opened my eyes, nothing had changed. My ears were still ringing and I still felt like eyes were boring into the back of my head.

I was dismayed. Her suggestion had sounded so easy, but I just couldn't do it.

"Can you help me get rid of them?" I asked.

I thought the process would be more complicated. At the very least, I thought she would wave her hands around me, chanting some ancient spell, but she didn't. She just gave me a long look, and the ghosts were gone in an instant. I could hear the sound of them receding into the distance until they disappeared with a faint pop.

I was relieved they were gone, but I couldn't still my lingering concern. If I picked those up so easily, surely more would follow. Some people thought the solution was simple. They suggested that I stop ghost hunting. The problem was: I wasn't just picking them up on ghost hunts. They were also finding me in restaurants, movie theaters, and in stores.

I couldn't understand why they were following. It wasn't as though I were outwardly inviting them along for the ride. Every time I felt one swoop in, I did everything possible to chase them away. After picking the brains of everyone I knew, I went back to the Internet to find some answers.

Through my research, I learned something that gave me a little insight, something that was confirmed later by another psychic medium friend. People who are sensitive to paranormal activity are like beacons to the spirit world. I don't know if we light up or emit some kind of glow they can see, but they are definitely attracted to us.

During investigations, I've noticed that ghosts often follow the strongest psychic in the group. We often divide into separate teams to contain the contamination from having too many people in one room. If one of the groups has a strong psychic among them, the other team can count on a quiet evening, similar to the one we'd just had the night before. Besides the one EVP, we came up empty.

This doesn't happen by accident. I believe that many of the ghosts still wandering around the earth are looking for help. When they see a psychic, they flock to them, hoping to find an answer for their problem.

Unfortunately, they were sometimes recognizing me as a psychic, but I couldn't help them. I knew they were there. I could hear them swirling around the room, but I couldn't communicate with them outside of using my paranormal equipment. And they really weren't utilizing my equipment either.

I've never understood this. If I were a ghost and a group of people wanted to know what it was like, I'd tell them. I'd have no hesitation. I'd spill my guts, unless...

"What if they can't? What if there are rules that prevent them from talking?" Sandy had asked me on more than one occasion.

It seemed like a logical answer, but it didn't quite fit every scenario. While we often get responses, many times they don't make any sense. It's as though they're not hearing us, and are simply spitting out words that don't go along with our conversation.

I've spent a long time wondering about this.

I think it must be very hard for a spirit to speak without a body to project the sound. It could be something that new ghosts have a hard time mastering. By the time they are old enough and strong enough, they've lost their desire to communicate with us. We're nothing more than nuisances, pestering them to answer asinine questions. And I also think they forget over time. The longer they're in our world in spirit form, the more their past lives fade away from them. It's only one theory though, and in truth, nobody really knows.

As the boat pulled away from the island, I watched the lighthouse recede into the distance. I needed to do something to change my fate. I couldn't keep living the way I was living. I made a promise to myself. When I got back, I was going to work on my book and find the success that had always eluded me. Just because bad things happened in the past, didn't mean I had to lie down and give up. I chose to fight for what I wanted.

I returned home from Rose Island thinking I was free of ghosts. I was actually excited to come back and literally have the house all to myself. There's something unsettling about having invisible houseguests hovering around you at all hours of the day or night. They would follow me into the bathroom, linger near me while I surfed the Internet, and they watched me as I watched TV. It was more than unnerving.

I walked through my doorway with a smile on my face, but it quickly faded as I heard the familiar sound of ear ringing. They were all waiting for me at my house. I hadn't gotten rid of a single one of them.

So much for the boat going out to sea. They just floated right back to my house and were hanging out, happy to have me back home again. I imagined them grinning, with their feet up on the coffee table, high-fiving one another.

I tried my best to ignore them. It was really the only option I had at my disposal. I was unable to push them away and sage didn't work. They seemed to like the smell. So, I just tried to ignore the ringing in my ears, and just went on with my life. Some of them drifted away on their own, but the majority of them didn't leave until I picked up the Soul Collector.

The minute he came into my life, my house emptied as if a ghost exterminator paid a visit.

Chapter 6

A few days after returning home from Rose Island, I received some great news I'd been eagerly waiting for. The tide seemed to be turning for me. Weeks earlier, I sent out nearly a hundred query letters to prospective literary agents, trying to find someone who would represent me, and help me sell my book, *Lightning Strikes*.

For years, if you didn't have an agent, you couldn't get your book published. And getting their attention was harder than being struck by lightning. They receive hundreds of letters every week, and only choose the ones that truly stood out to them.

It really was an unfair procedure. I'd read many books that were poorly written that had somehow gotten published. Why couldn't I get mine onto the bookshelves?

Every writer hopes to get the kind of email I received. A literary agency just outside of New York contacted me, telling me that my book sounded interesting, and they wanted to read the entire manuscript. I was the envy of my writer friends.

This was huge.

I spent the next few weeks pouring over my manuscript, trying to make it as perfect as possible. Was it thrilling enough? Was it written well? Would they like it?

Being a published author had been my dream since high school.

I grew up in the back woods of Southern Indiana. When I was eight years old, my parents divorced, and I lived with my mother. She eventually remarried, so we moved to a nice house in the country. Like the mother-daughter relationship I now share with my own daughter, my mother and I had a hard time getting along. After a big fight, I announced that I was going to go live with my father.

The move wasn't an easy one. I left all my friends behind, and changed schools in my junior year of high school. I knew a few people, because I went to grade school with many of them before my parent's divorce, but it was still very awkward trying to fit in.

I eventually found my place in a creative writing class.

The teacher of the class was a motherly, but tough woman. I worried about turning in my first essay. Was it good enough? Would she like it? The answer was yes to both questions. She took my essay and read it to all of her other classes, sparking something inside me that would continue to grow.

By the time I received the email from the literary agency, I'd already written six other novels. I went through the long, nail-biting process of trying to find an agent for each one. Each time, I would catch someone's interest, only to have them shoot me down after several months of waiting. I would put the manuscript in the closet with the others and vow to write something better next time.

I had high hopes for *Lightning Strikes* though. I spent a full year working on it, and it was the best thing I'd ever written. I kept my fingers crossed as I emailed this new agent.

Surely, it was time for something good to happen to me.

In the meantime, my elation over my book competed with the lingering depression over my failed relationship. What did I do with my time?

We had a regular routine that we followed. On Thursdays, I went to his apartment after I finished working for the day. We'd have dinner, watch a movie, and just spend time together. I'd drive home the next morning, work for the day, and then return to his apartment for the weekend. Now, my days came without direction, and Thursdays were a nightmare.

I came to a turning point one Friday night. I realized that it was truly over between us. There was no going back. After a weak moment, I emailed him the good news about the literary agent. I got back a terse response, telling me I was crazy and that I thought I had super-powers.

There was just no going back. It was done. It was over.

I spent the majority of that Saturday on the couch, watching an endless line of television shows, and crying about my lonely life. Everyone I knew bounced back from failed relationships fairly quickly, finding the love of their life within months. I felt like perhaps this wasn't in the cards for me.

Maybe, I was meant to spend my life alone.

I began to fantasize about becoming a crazy cat lady. I pictured myself sitting in my house until I was old and feeble, with dozens of cats perched on every chair and counter.

Then I got a phone call that changed everything.

It was one of my friends calling to ask. "Do you want to go to the Prison Camp tonight?" Suddenly my mood went from somber to excited. "Yes!" was the answer. As it turns out, I should have stayed on my couch crying.

This would be the night I would meet the Soul Collector.

(Below) Solitary confinement buildings at the Prison Camp

(Below) Remnants of the root cellar built at the Prison Camp

Chapter 7

The Prison Camp is located in a remote area, far from the nearest human inhabitant. The road leading to it was overgrown and rutted, but the stars above us shone brighter and clearer than I'd ever witnessed before. It was our favorite place to investigate.

Built in the early nineteen hundreds, it was a working prison that housed prisoners serving moderate sentences for minor offenses. Photos from the time period show men working the fields and caring for the many animals.

Besides the actual prison itself, there were many other buildings to explore. There was a dormitory, dairy barn, and sawmill, as well as a root cellar built into the side of a hill. While it was active, prisoners worked the one-hundred-fifty acre farm, producing enough milk, beef, and vegetables to sustain the prison without the need for additional funding.

Years later, during the outbreak of tuberculosis, they added a thirty-bed hospital down the road, bringing in sick patients from all over the state. Not all of these later prisoners were of the milder variety. Many were shipped in from local prisons, where they were serving time for much more serious crimes.

The Prison Camp was abandoned in 1934, because the property was located on the drainage area of a water supply that fed into a local reservoir being built. The property now stands in ruins.

After finding maps on the Internet earlier in the summer, my ghost hunting friends Tina Aube, Keith Glenn, and I spent months exploring the overgrowth, while trying to find each building on the map. Most of the buildings were reduced down to stone foundations. We were able to locate most of them, intrigued at the way time had deteriorated the mammoth structures down to mere footprints.

We brought our friends to see it, conducting dozens of investigations over the course of the summer.

While the farmland and prison camp area seemed fairly benign, we had a different experience at the foundation of the old TB hospital. It had a somber feeling to it. You could stand there in the middle of it, and just feel the past vibrating under your feet. We quickly took out our recorders, and began our attempts to talk to the dead.

Over the period of a few months, we became well versed on the property's history. During the Revolutionary War, the property had also served as a prisoner of war camp. Both British and German prisoners of war were kept there, many of whom were forced to march a long distance just to get there.

I marveled at what they went through, asking them what it was like to finally get to the camp after such a horrific journey, where many of them died in transit.

"It must have been like Heaven, after everything you went through to get here," I said.

The response was appropriate. "Don't it," a ghostly presence answered.

https://soundcloud.com/jonimayhan/dont-it
(EVP available on Soundcloud.com/jonimayhan)

Who were the people who lingered here? Were they once prisoners of war, or were they the men who had to work off a sentence for public intoxication?

We asked, but weren't sure of the answer. They simply said no.

https://soundcloud.com/jonimayhan/solitary-cell-4-were-you-kept
(EVP available on Soundcloud.com/jonimayhan)

The response only elicited more questions. So, who then? And, what were they feeling? Did they feel sad? Were they feeling as cold as we were?

One thing was certain: there was plenty of activity there. We spent a lot of time walking around the TB hospital ruins, dodging the thick undergrowth and prickly thorns, hoping for a paranormal experience. At one point, my EMF meter rose to 2.4. This was pretty astounding to us considering there were no electrical sources within five miles of the location. We watched it rise and then fall again, only to increase a few more times before returning to zero. A normal reading for the Prison Camp would have been zero, so this was interesting for us.

We found an old ceramic-coated bowl sitting on a post. One of the investigators pulled it off to look at it. Apparently, this wasn't something the resident ghosts appreciated.

"Hey, put it back," they told us.

https://soundcloud.com/jonimayhan/tb-hospital-hey-put-it-back-1
(EVP available on Soundcloud.com/jonimayhan)

This particular night, things just seemed different. It was a feeling all of us had. The entire mood of the camp had changed. It felt darker and more menacing. I kept looking over my shoulder, getting the distinct feeling someone was following us.

As we sat in the root cellar, doing an EVP session, we kept seeing shadows move across the walls.

"Did you see that?" my friend, Tina said, pointing towards a dark wall. The entire root cellar was like a cave. While the walls were made of cement, the entire structure had been built into the side of a hill. The only light we could see came from the opening, which was nearly obscured with vines and brush.

I looked to where she was pointing. The air seemed to be swirling and churning. If I stared hard enough, I could see the movement she was talking about. We weren't alone, and we all knew it.

As the night grew late, the air developed a definite chill to it. The ghosts seemed to grow a little edgier, as well.

One of them agreed with us about the temperature. She told us that it was cold in there.

https://soundcloud.com/jonimayhan/its-cold-in-here
(EVP available on Soundcloud.com/jonimayhan)

We continued another EVP session at the TB hospital foundation, quickly finding a spirit who wanted to talk with us.

"What do you want us to do?" I asked.

"Fall," was the answer. It wasn't very reassuring.

https://soundcloud.com/jonimayhan/fall
(EVP available on Soundcloud.com/jonimayhan)

"What are you doing here?" I asked again.

The answer came swiftly: "Following."

https://soundcloud.com/jonimayhan/sets/soul-collector
(EVP available on Soundcloud.com/jonimayhan)

After about nine p.m., the activity died down, as it often did at that location. We always wondered about this. Why would they settle down every night at the same time? Was it the time when the prison turned the lights out for the night? Or, was there somewhere else they needed to be? We weren't sure. All we knew was that the place literally emptied out every evening and we would be lucky to get even a single hit on our equipment.

This was one of the last EVPs I captured there. The male voice was familiar, since he'd been speaking to me in several other audio captures. The whispery voice sounds like he's saying "Can't stop breathing," then something else I can't understand.

I left the Prison Camp that night with an uneasy feeling. My ears were ringing all the way home, which wasn't a very comforting sensation. It usually meant that someone was still with me.

I stopped the car in the middle of the dirt road.

"Whoever you are, you need to go back to where you came from. You are forbidden to follow me," I demanded.

I pulled out a bundle of sage I carried in my equipment bag, and lit it with trembling fingers. The sweet smell of sage rose into the air, the wisps of smoke looking like apparitions in the clear, dark night. By the time I got home, the ringing was softer, but I wasn't convinced I was truly alone.

This would be when it would all begin, when my life took a hellish turn.

(Below) Graffiti inside the root cellar

(Below) Sandy MacLeod and Stephen Flaherty inside the root cellar

Chapter 8

When I got home, I had a strange feeling that just wouldn't leave me.

I felt it the minute I came through the door. I couldn't put my finger on what was bothering me, but something just wasn't right.

I flipped on light switches as I made my way through the house, chasing away the darkness. My dog trotted along behind me, giving me curious looks. Surely, if someone had broken in while I was gone she'd be acting differently.

Ripley wasn't guard dog material, but she was very protective of the house. If someone came up to the door, she'd start barking. She'd never let someone in without a battle.

I finally just came back into the living room and plopped down on the couch. The front door had been locked and nothing was out of place. So why was I feeling so edgy?

I flipped through the channels on my TV, hoping to find something to watch before bedtime. I've always been a fan of paranormal shows, but I bypassed them. If I was already creeped out, watching a ghost show probably wouldn't help me. After a while, I just gave up and decided to go to bed.

I walked into my bedroom and the sensation grew much stronger.

My ears began ringing with an odd tone, one I'd never heard before. Had something followed me home from the Prison Camp? I looked around the room, studying the corners.

"If somebody is here, you need to leave. You can't stay here," I said.

The ear ringing continued, so I pulled out my bundle of sage.

Even though I'd just smudged my car, I also smudged the entire house, making sure I allowed the smoke to permeate through every square inch of the structure. After I was finished, I felt a little better, but I wasn't sure I'd done anything productive. I could still hear a tone.

Something about the tone bothered me. It wasn't the high-pitch I often heard. It had a lower register, almost sounding like static. It wasn't something I'd ever heard before, and that alone bothered me. Had I picked someone up at the Prison Camp?

"You need to go back to the Prison Camp. There's nothing for you here," I said again.

I went to bed, but had a hard time falling asleep. Every time I closed my eyes, I felt as though someone was standing beside me. I used to work with a guy who amused himself by sneaking up on me, then hovering directly behind me until I sensed he was there. I'd turn around with a start, before swatting him. This feeling was much the same.

I opened my eyes, time after time, only to find the room empty. My dog was camped out on the floor beside my bed and didn't seem disturbed by anything. I should have been watching my cats instead.

Normally, my cats claimed the two bottom corners of my bed, staying well out of kicking range. I often tossed and turned in my sleep, and they knew where the safe zones were. This night they were nowhere in sight.

Exhaustion finally claimed me and I finally fell into a restless asleep.

The next morning, the sun was shining brightly through the windows. It was a beautiful October morning. The trees were aglow with festive orange and yellow leaves. I hopped out of bed, eager to start the day. The night's eeriness faded away with the break of dawn.

I sat down at my laptop, determined to review all of my audio. Most people don't appreciate the effort a paranormal investigator goes through for an investigation. For every hour we investigate, we have to come home and listen to the entire recorded session again to see if we captured any documentation of a haunting. If I find something, I'll section off the area on the audio, and then save it as a clip. My friends were always impatient to hear what I'd found, so I made it a point to always post my EVPs the day after an investigation.

I uploaded the audio recordings from my digital recorder to my laptop, and then began the arduous task of listening to it through my headphones. At first, I was just happy to have captured some very clear responses. Then, I began noticing a pattern. The same male voice was on many of the EVPS.

It made the hair on the back of my neck stand up. Had he been following us, like he said on the EVP? Was he still following me?

I tried to shake it off, but the feeling of being watched grew so strong I couldn't ignore it. My ears started ringing even stronger, and I began to get mental images of a very scary man frowning at me, looming behind me.

This was different from the other hitchhikers. Normally, I could hear and feel their presence, but couldn't get a sense of who they were. They were just sounds that followed me around, causing me to look nervously over my shoulder. With him, it was different.

I spent the day cleaning and catching up with household tasks, but the feeling of being watched just wouldn't leave me. Was I just creeping myself out, or was there something actually there with me?

By bedtime, I was more than a little unnerved. I walked into my bedroom and a sound exploded just to my right. It was as though someone pounded on the wall with a heavy fist. I jumped, barely stifling a scream. As I reached my nightstand, to put my cell phone on the charger, another bang sounded again beside me.

"Please just leave me alone," I pleaded with the unseen entity. "If I did something that offended you, I'm truly sorry."

I searched the air, seeing nothing. Somehow, I managed to drift off to sleep, awakening the next morning with the same sense of doom and gloom haunting me.

I walked into the kitchen to make a pot of coffee. I'd just filled the pot with water when I heard another bang on the wall beside me. I jumped, nearly dropping the pot.

"Go away!" I said, not knowing where to look in the room.

I could literally feel his anger. Words began floating in my mind. I could feel him berating me all through the day, judgmental and angry.

Something had followed me and it wasn't nice.

As the days progressed, he became bolder. The wall pounding grew more consistent. The thoughts became more pronounced, as though I were hearing someone else's voice inside the confines of my own head.

If I dropped something on the floor, I could hear him in my mind, calling me clumsy. I walked past a full trash can, and he told me I was lazy for not emptying it. He made it clear that he didn't like my pets, especially my cats. He thought they made too much of a mess.

Was I losing my mind? Wasn't that what happened to crazy people? They heard voices in their heads.

I didn't like this new turn of events at all. I wanted him out of my house and, especially, out of my head.

Over the course of a week, my mood became dark. I lost track of time, finding myself sleepwalking at night, something I hadn't done in years. I became jumpy. The least little thing scared me. I spent a lot of time glancing over my shoulder. I hardly slept at all.

My bedroom became a torture chamber. The minute I walked in, I could feel him there, standing in the corner of the room. I started seeing movements out of the corner of my eye. By the time I'd turn around, it would be gone. I began hearing more strange sounds throughout the house. I'd turn off a lamp, only to find it turned back on again, moments later. Suddenly ghost hunting didn't sound like such a great idea.

What had I messed with?

It just kept getting worse. During the following week, my cats began watching something float into the room, and then drift over the top of my bed. They both stared with the same intensity as if they were watching a housefly, except it was early winter, and there weren't any bugs. I tried to debunk it. I looked for a possible explanation, but couldn't find one.

I had picked up another unwanted hitchhiker.

I smudged my house with sage frequently, filling my house with the rich smell of burning herbs. I followed up by telling the entity to leave. I prayed, asking for protection. I recited the Saint Michael's Prayer. I did everything I could think of, but nothing worked. He hovered menacingly over my shoulder, making my life miserable.

I told a few friends, but for the most part, I just kept it to myself.

If I started talking about having a ghostly attachment, I was worried that people would think I was crazy. I tried to maintain a normal existence, and continued living my life as if nothing horrible was happening to me. I posted happy, silly things on Facebook, worked feverishly on *Lightning Strikes*, and spent time with my nearly grown children. I wouldn't understand what was truly happening to me until I began spending time with our team's psychic medium.

Then, it would only get worse.

Chapter 9

Halloween has always been my favorite holiday.

It is the time of year when the world celebrates the paranormal. Television stations broadcast my favorite horror movies, and paranormal shows play back-to-back episodes.

When my children were younger, I used to decorate my yard with gravestones and floating ghosts. One year, we set up a haunted walk in the woods behind our house, employing our neighbors as ghouls, ghosts, and chainsaw-toting madmen. Now, I had my own resident ghost who was turning my home into a true haunted house.

I wasn't feeling my normal enthusiasm for the season, but I still decorated the house. I hung graveyard netting on my kitchen window, and even painted a mural of a graveyard on the glass below it. I adorned the windowsill with fake rats and flying bats. I stopped myself short of hanging fake ghosts from the ceiling. Somehow, that just didn't seem appropriate, given my current situation.

I didn't have any plans, and my house didn't get very many trick-or-treaters, something I truly missed. My choices were simple: I could sit around and keep my unwanted house guest entertained, or I could find something else to do. When I was invited to help with an event at my favorite haunted house, I jumped at the opportunity. It would provide me with a pleasant distraction.

The SK Pierce Mansion, located in Gardner, Massachusetts, has always been a favorite of mine. Before I even knew it was haunted, I used to drive past it, and stare up at the mammoth structure, wondering if anyone was looking back at me. I had become friends with the owners over the past few years and was happy to help them with their charity haunted house event.

We spent several evenings decorating the 6,000 square foot gothic Victorian, hanging ghouls from the ceilings, and cobwebs in the corners. We planned to have a tour of the mansion on the Saturday before Halloween. Unfortunately for us, Mother Nature had other plans. The night before the event, we received an unexpected two feet of snow.

Not having access to a snow blower, I was forced to spend the day shoveling my driveway by hand, cursing at the plow as he drove by and deposited more snow in my driveway. By the time the event was due to start, I was exhausted, but determined to get there.

The roads were rough. Because the trees were still heavy with leaves, the snow knocked down many limbs, pulling the power lines down as they fell. Thankfully, I made it to the Victorian safely and was thrilled to see they had power. The event was on.

Despite the weather, people were lined up all the way down the street, waiting to come inside. It was evident that people were eager to visit the grand Victorian. Many of them were locals, wanting to get a peek at the interior, like I was years ago. The house was a local legend, and for a good reason.

The owner often invited ghost hunting teams to come in and investigate. I'd been there many times before, and always found it intriguing. The spirits were, for the most part, kind and generous with their communication. I never left without getting at least one good EVP.

Unlike many other places I'd investigated, the spirits there often responded with very intelligent answers, letting us know they were not only aware of us, but also aware of their surroundings.

When we asked what town one of our investigators lived in, a spirit responded with "She lives in Gardner."

https://soundcloud.com/jonimayhan/stairs-she-lives-in-gardner
(EVP available on Soundcloud.com/jonimayhan)

Another known spirit in the house is Maddie, a nanny who lived in the house in the late 1800's and cared for the Pierce children. When we asked if she was there, she responded with, "Come talk to me. Come talk to me."

https://soundcloud.com/jonimayhan/stairs-maddie-are-you-here
(EVP available on Soundcloud.com/jonimayhan)

The mansion had many intriguing rooms, including the Red Room, where a prostitute had reportedly been murdered, and the master bedroom, where a man once self-combusted after an evening of drinking moonshine in bed. But for the tour, I'd be spending the entire evening in the basement.

If there is a place in the Victorian that isn't as friendly as the rest, it would be the basement. Many spirits hang out down there, but one in particular gets the most attention. People always call him a negative entity, but I had other thoughts about him. He made it clear that he didn't like people tromping through the house, disrupting him. In my mind, he was no different than a grumpy old man who was tired of all the commotion. I respected his wishes. When he was finished with us and wanted us to leave, he had a very distinct way of telling us. He'd fill the room with anger, giving me a bad vibe I couldn't ignore. I would comply by ending the session, and moving my team to another area of the house.

Even the resident spirits in the house seem apprehensive about the entity in the basement. I captured this response on my Spirit Box at a prior investigation.

We asked if the spirits were afraid of the entity in the basement. One responded, "The devil".

https://soundcloud.com/jonimayhan/billiards-room-ghost-box-1

(EVP available on Soundcloud.com/jonimayhan)

I went downstairs ahead of everyone else. It may have sounded foolish, but I wanted to prep the resident ghosts for what was ahead of them.

I informed the spirits about the tour, telling them that the funds were needed for the upkeep of the house. Built in 1875, the house was starting to show its age. The roof leaked, and the eaves were pulling away from the structure. If something wasn't done soon, there wouldn't be a house left for them to haunt.

I don't know if they understood me or not, but when I came down the stairs an hour later, they didn't protest. I imagined them slinking to the farthest corners of the room, watching us with horrified expressions on their ghostly faces.

Over thirty volunteers ended up working the event. My group, "the basement dwellers", as I came to call them, did an outstanding job. A guy, who was dressed up like Freddy from the horror movie, leapt out of a doorway as people passed by. When the guests walked into a darker section of the basement, they were greeted by Scream and our resident ghoul. While they were appropriately terrifying, the scariest person in the basement was the clown.

Clowns have never bothered me, but as I walked into the room where he hid, he nearly scared me to death. I never knew where he was going to hide. Sometimes, he was behind a curtain, and other times behind a door. When he jumped out and screamed, I usually screamed along with the guests. Maybe it had something to do with my current mental state, but having someone jump out and scare me wasn't on my current wish list.

By the end of the night, we'd had over four-hundred people pass through the tour. I was pleasantly exhausted. It was the most fun I'd had in a very long while. I wasn't looking forward to going back home to my own haunted house, though.

"Wish me luck," I told the Victorian spirits, and then headed home.

I was greeted by dark windows and a driveway full of snow, thanks to the snowplows. I just drove over the top of the mound of snow, before going inside to spend the night with a negative entity, in a house with no power.

(Below) the SK Pierce house (aka: The Haunted Victorian Mansion) in Gardner, MA

Chapter 10

Halloween came and went with little fanfare. The fun I had at the Victorian would be all I'd enjoy for the season.

Too afraid to rock the boat with my resident spirit, I stayed away from the scary movies I had enjoyed in the past. It just didn't seem worth the risk. I passed the time working on my book, and resisting the urge to look over my shoulder every three seconds.

My family would call me frequently, worried.

"Are you okay?" they'd ask, thinking I was still sad about my recent breakup with my boyfriend. By this time, I missed the companionship, but was far more concerned with the paranormal activities going on in my house. I told them I was fine, and then tried hard to sound more cheerful the next time they called.

Truthfully, I wasn't ready to share my experiences with them. They would have believed me, but I didn't want them to worry. I was doing enough of that for all of us. I knew they worried about my ghost hunting. At first, they'd been apprehensive about the stories I shared, but after they listened to my EVPs they became believers.

I was often worried that people from my childhood would think I'd gone off the deep end. While they were sharing stories about their fabulous vacations, and pictures of their grandchildren, I was wandering around in abandoned asylums, looking for trouble.

As November progressed, I began to think about the holidays. Thanksgiving was a very depressing holiday for me. I had nowhere to go. My family was a thousand miles away, and my kids were spending the holiday with their father's family. I didn't want to spend the day by myself.

Thanksgiving is a family day. It's a time when loved ones get together, while the tantalizing smell of turkey and pie fills the air. It is a day filled with laughter and shared stories. It isn't a time for negative entities.

Past years, I loaded my dog into the car, and headed for Indiana to spend the day with my family. This year that just wasn't an option. I just didn't have the energy for it. Eighteen hours on the road, with nothing to think about but my miseries, wasn't my idea of a good time. Besides, I couldn't put my family in danger. What if he decided he liked them better and stayed? I couldn't take that risk.

I put out a very needy plea on Facebook, asking if anyone had room at their table for me, and my wish was quickly granted. I was invited to spend the holiday with Jennifer Julian and her family, along with several of my ghost hunting friends in Maine.

I made the trek, trying not to think about all that I had lost, but I couldn't help it. After nineteen-years of marriage, I had spent five lonely years trying to find my place in this world. I thought I'd finally found it and had embraced all the opportunities, only to find myself completely alone again. I wasn't sure I was up for the challenge. Having to spend a family-oriented holiday with near strangers seemed like the end of the world to me. And, then it got worse.

Much worse.

One fun night of ghost hunting at the Prison Camp would haunt me for months.

I had to wonder if it was even worth it. Should I just give up ghost hunting for good? As it turns out, I wouldn't have a choice in the matter.

When I didn't hunt for the ghosts, they began hunting me.

(Below) Tina Aube and Keith Glenn inside the TB hospital foundation in 2011

(Below) Joni with Steven Flaherty, Jimmy Bennett, and Michael Cram at the Prison Camp 2011

(Below) Joni investigating Solitary Confinement at the Prison Camp

Chapter 11

I had another reason to drive to Maine for Thanksgiving. The psychic medium from our team would be there. I wanted to see what she thought about my latest spirit attachment.

I walked through the doorway, a gust of wintery air blowing leaves in behind me. She took one look at me and said four words that nearly rocked my world off its axis.

"We need to talk," she told me.

That was when I learned that my suspicions were right. I did have a negative entity that was following me around. What she said next would leave me with nightmares for months.

"It's bad. Really bad," she told me. "He's a soul collector, and he has his sights set on you."

Everyone was anxious to start eating, so she told me that we'd talk later. As I sat around the table, passing the stuffing, corn, and mashed potato bowls, I couldn't stop thinking about what she told me. What was a soul collector? I'd never heard the term before.

In my mind, I began conjuring up gruesome imagines. I imagined a spindly specter, with stringy grey hair hanging from his skull. Around his neck, he would wear a necklace laced with ears from the souls he'd collected.

"Joni, can you pass the gravy?" someone asked me, tugging me from my inner nightmare.

Somehow we made it through dinner. After the dishes were washed, and the kitchen was tidied up, I found the psychic medium again. I couldn't wait any longer. I needed to know what I was dealing with.

She took me to a quiet part of the room.

"Don't worry. We'll get rid of him. I just want you to know what you're dealing with," she told me.

"He's a soul collector?" I asked. "What is that exactly?"

She took a deep breath, before giving something over my shoulder another long inspection. "Well, when I look at him, I see people gathered behind him. They just go on and on."

"How many?" I asked, but she just arched her eyebrows, apparently not wanting to tell me the bad news. "Hundreds?" I guessed.

"At least that many," was all she said.

"They look sick too. Did you just investigate at an old hospital?" she asked.

I felt my stomach clinch. While I had told her about investigating at the Prison Camp, I hadn't had a chance to tell her about the old TB hospital nearby. The fact that she was picking up on this was disconcerting.

There was no doubt in my mind that she knew what she was doing. Previously, she'd worked with the state police, helping them with missing person claims. She often told us about dreams she had that eventually came true as well. One was especially chilling.

She had a dream that children were trapped inside of a house. She saw gas cans and fire sprouting out all around them. A month later, a man killed his children by lighting his house on fire with gasoline. I'd heard about her dream before the actual event, which stilled any doubts I might have had. She was the real deal.

I told her about the old TB hospital. We'd spent most of the summer exploring the area. I'd been there dozens of times without an issue. Why would this happen now? Did I make one of them angry? I'm always very respectful of spirits when I investigate. I always ask them if they need help, and I never provoke them just to get a response. It didn't make sense.

"Why would they follow me?" I asked.

It was then that I learned my fate in life.

"You're a beacon," she said, solemnly.

"Is it because I'm a sensitive?" I asked. She nodded.

I already knew I was a sensitive. This wasn't news to me, but it made everything else come together in my mind.

Sensitives are people who are able to sense ghosts or spirits. Some just feel the ghosts move into the room, others have physical cues like a tingling on the back of their necks, or goose bumps that rise up on their arms. My clairaudient abilities were just the tip of what I was capable of and I knew it. I was afraid to allow myself to develop any further.

'You're in a state of transition right now. If you continue to work with it, your ability will get stronger," she told me. I wasn't sure whether to be happy or afraid.

I'd spent enough time with her to know that being a psychic is both a blessing and a curse. We couldn't go anywhere without her being hounded by the dead. Once, while we were at a restaurant, she stopped eating and just sat there, staring into the air.

"Give me a minute," she told us, getting up from the table. She came back minutes later to tell us that she had to pass a message onto one of the cooks in the kitchen. Apparently, his partner had died months earlier, and needed to pass along a message. It would happen everywhere she went. It wasn't something I wanted for myself.

She must have understood my conflict, because she spent some time, trying to teach me how to push the spirits away from me. It was a very good first step. I tried to visualize a white light surrounding me, keeping me protected, but I couldn't hold the visualization for more than a few seconds before my mind wandered to other things. She told me to keep practicing, that I would need it.

Despite what she taught me, I couldn't seem to master the ability. I felt as though I were trying to climb a hill on roller skates. Every time I felt like I was making progress, I'd slip back down to the bottom. Something that came so easily for her and other psychics wasn't so simple for me. Until I'd learned how to push the spirits away, I would continue to be a target for them.

She promised to help me with the negative attachment, and sent me on my way.

"Don't worry. I'll help you with this. We'll figure it all out," she said.

I pulled on my coat and braced myself for the cold. Day had turned to night while I was inside, and I wasn't thrilled with the change. Gone was the sunny, warm feeling of Thanksgiving. In its place was something much darker and far more sinister.

It was a long drive home, hearing his signature tone in the car with me. I felt a sense of panic rising inside of me. How could I live like this, knowing an evil entity was lurking over my shoulder? How would I even begin to tuck myself into bed and close my eyes? I was terrified.

I researched the subject as much as I could, learning things that only made me more anxious. I was initially skeptical about the concept of a soul collector, but the more I read, the more I became convinced.

Supposedly, negative entities do sometimes collect other souls. In some cultures, they are known to do this in order to achieve a higher rank in the spirit world. I slept very little, often retreating to the couch in the living room where it felt a bit safer.

Why me?

Seriously, this guy could have picked on any number of people. The place I investigated was popular with many paranormal investigators. Ghost hunters were in and out of there on a regular basis.

The days passed by slowly. I couldn't sleep and I couldn't talk about it. My teenage son, Trevor, lived with me four days a week, compounding the situation.

Trevor wasn't the kind of person who scared easily, but he'd never expressed any interest in my paranormal fixations. He made it clear that he didn't want to hear about my ghost hunts. He'd listen politely for a while, and then quickly change the subject. I didn't want to scare him with what was happening to me. But on the other hand, I didn't want to endanger him either. What was I going to do?

Towards the middle of the week, I couldn't take it any longer. The entity seemed to be latching onto me even tighter, never leaving me alone for even a minute during the day or night. I called the psychic medium again.

"Why me?" I asked, not really expecting an answer. I'd been picking up spirit attachments frequently for the past year. While most eventually drifted away, probably bored with their host, this one seemed to be making a permanent home just behind my shoulder.

"It probably had something to do with your overall wellbeing when you went there," she told me.

I sunk back into my couch, the cell phone nearly falling from my fingers. She knew about the breakup with my boyfriend. She was with me at Rose Island just after it happened. While I didn't tell everyone about it, word still got around. Some ghost hunters are lucky and have understanding partners who share the hobby with them. Others, like me, seemed to have a harder time.

It was the true definition of insult after injury. The depression from my break up left me in a more vulnerable state. I'd let my guard down, which allowed this entity access to me.

Great.

"He wants you," she told me. "Whenever I see him, I see him standing over your shoulder, whispering in your ear. Can you hear him?" she asked.

I could just hear the ear-shattering buzz that followed me through all the hours of my days and nights, but I didn't know if the voice in my head were real or imagined. Knowing that he was constantly with me nearly sent me off the deep end. He followed me into the bathroom, was always lurking close as I showered and dressed. He hovered over my bed all night long, just inches away from my face. He wasn't letting me go.

"He wants you all to himself," she told me. "He keeps telling me that you're his."

Every cell in my body went into red alert. I held my breath as the news sunk in.

She promised to continue helping me, pulling him off of me when she could.

The relief couldn't come soon enough.

Chapter 12

It was as if he knew he was under attack. He began fighting back in earnest. He wanted to cut me off from everyone, so he started with my electronics. I suddenly began having issues with my Internet connection and my cell phone. I would call someone, and the line would become filled with static. Sometimes it wouldn't work at all. My phone would go dead, and nothing short of rebooting it would get it to work again. Not only was I terrified, this entity was systematically cutting me off from the rest of the world, from the help I so desperately needed.

Then, it escalated even further. My phone wouldn't ring at all if certain people tried to call me. Telemarketers always got through, as did my veterinarian, reminding me about my dog's next appointment. The calls that wouldn't show up were the ones from my friends who wanted to help me. I wouldn't realize they called unless they left a voice mail message. That was one thing he wasn't capable of stopping.

"I've called you several times," Sandy said one day. "I was worried about you."

The psychic medium had already warned my friends that he might try to sequester me. She said that if he couldn't cut me off, he might attempt to alter my moods, making me want to stay home alone. She told my friends to call me frequently, and try to get me out of the house as often as possible. It seemed very strange in the beginning, because I'm not the type to be so easily persuaded. Was he really capable of altering my decisions? Later, I came to realize just how accurate she really was.

It was beginning to feel like I was living in my own prison. Someone was trying to make all my decisions for me, deciding who I was allowed to talk to, and who I wasn't. I didn't like it one bit.

I knew I was being a pest, but I kept reaching out to the psychic medium, asking if she could come to my house, offering to pay her way, offering anything I could think of to get this entity off me. Unfortunately, she was going through issues of her own with family and work. She kept telling me she would help me, but as the days went by I began to lose hope. I fell into an even deeper fugue that I just couldn't emerge from.

I've always been the kind of person who bounces back quickly. I've never suffered from depression, or had anything truly get me down for more than a day. I usually wake up the next morning determined to conquer what is ailing me. This time, there didn't seem to be any hope.

I'm thankful I had great friends as I was going through this. Since they were also ghost hunters, I didn't have to prove I wasn't crazy. They knew that what I was dealing with was real. They listened to my stories, offered me couches and spare beds to sleep on, and tried to help me figure it all out.

My friend, Tina Aube, invited me over to her apartment to watch movies and play games. Even though she was new to the paranormal world, she was an eager student. We talked about the Soul Collector for hours, comparing him to other situations we had encountered. Nothing else even came close. We were used to going to a location, investigating for a few hours, and then going home to review our audio. Nothing of this magnitude had ever happened to us before.

Unfortunately, I could find very little information about it.

I went back to the Internet for information to try to find out more information about spirit attachments. I found several cases that were somewhat similar, but none that matched it closely. Even though I felt him looming over my shoulder, I began to doubt the information the psychic medium gave me. Maybe, he wasn't a soul collector. Maybe, he was just a negative spirit who was presenting himself as something worse.

This had happened to us before. Ghosts could be deliberately deceptive. They could project any image they want to, and they weren't always honest. Sometimes, they led us in the wrong direction, as if playing with us.

"Are you a woman?" we'd ask. The flashlight would light up.

"Are you a man?" I'd ask, just wanting to double-back and confirm the first answer. The flashlight would come back on again.

"Well, you can't be both," I'd muse, wondering if the ghosts were deceiving us, or our methods weren't dependable.

Frankly, I wasn't completely convinced that the flashlight method was an accurate way of hunting for ghosts. It seemed fishy to me that it only worked with flashlights that twisted on and off. Why wouldn't it work with push button versions?

I saw a video on the Internet that confirmed my suspicions. It was long and rambling; full of technical jargon that went over my head, but it explained the phenomena, and gave it a rational spin. When you turn a flashlight in between the on and off position, it causes the battery to arc. This creates a temporary weld that cools, and then heats back up again, making a momentary connection that turns on the flashlight. After learning that information, I couldn't trust the flashlight method any longer.

My friends would grow weary with my frequent skepticism.

"Watch," Sandy would tell me. "The light comes on right after I ask a question."

Surely, this couldn't be coincidence? Or a temporary weld. Other friends would show me video footage of a flashlight sitting on a bed. For over an hour it would remain in the off position, only to start flicking on and off once an investigator came into the room, and began asking questions.

I bowed a little on my skepticism. "Okay, then prove me wrong," I told the spirits. "If the answer is yes, turn the flashlight on once. If the answer is no, turn it on twice." I've yet to have this happen.

After the Soul Collector came to stay with me, I'd soon change my opinion on this.

I had a flashlight sitting on my kitchen counter. I didn't pay any attention to it. It was just there in case of an emergency. All of a sudden, it started flicking on and off all by itself.

"Are you the man who's been following me?" I asked.

The light came on brightly. My heart nearly skipped a beat.

While I was curious about him, I was warned to NEVER investigate inside my own house. Friends told me it gave the spirits more reasons to stay. Many times, they follow sensitives because they want help, or are looking for a human experience. If I was unable to help them, it was better to convince them to move along to somewhere else. The same rules applied to the Soul Collector. If I wanted him to leave, I had to make sure I wasn't providing him with more motivation.

In retrospect, I really wish I had better documented the experience. I ran my recorder all night one night, hoping to learn more about him, but my friends pleaded with me to erase it. They didn't want me to do anything that could hamper our efforts to remove him.

I saw their point. Why take any chances? I ended up erasing it, afraid to do something wrong.

The activity continued, despite my will to stop it. It didn't seem to matter what I did. He made it clear he wasn't finished with me.

One day while I was working, my cell phone suddenly came on and began playing music. I sat stock-still and stared at it.

Was this really happening?

In order to turn my phone on, I had to push, and then slide a button. To play music, I had to scroll through the apps to find the music icon. Then, I'd have to press the play button. He'd done this all by himself.

The worst part was his song choice. "Addicted," by Saving Abel. It's a song about a man who is emotionally and sexually addicted to a woman, not the kind of song I wanted a negative entity serenading me with.

It hit me on two levels, something I'm sure he was well aware of.

I used to burn CDs for my ex-boyfriend, selecting songs that made me think about him. This was one of the songs on the last CD I burned for him, and it brought me back to a place where I didn't want to go.

I shut my phone off and just stared into space.

Emotionally, I was shutting down. I didn't sleep more than a few hours a night. I stopped eating. I lost fifteen pounds, which wasn't something that has ever been easy for me, and I started smoking again. I'd given it up years earlier, but there I was lighting up again. I was quickly moving from depression to oppression, something I wouldn't understand until I reached out to another friend, Michael Cram.

Michael is a fellow paranormal investigator. Tall and thin, he carries a fatherly air of confidence with him that I have always found reassuring. If I had a question about an investigation, he always had an answer for me. His wife Nancy often went with him.

He was studying with the Catholic Church on the practice of exorcism. If someone had a claim of demonic possession, the local church called him in to investigate. He would go in with his friend, Steven Flaherty, to check it out. If he felt it was a true possession, and had enough documentation to back up the claims, he would call the church to perform an exorcism.

Michael, Steven, and Nancy showed up at my house the day after I called. They literally dropped everything to help me.

"Hey kiddo," he said, greeting me at the door.

I couldn't have been happier to see him. If the psychic medium angle wasn't working on the Soul Collector, maybe Michael could convince God to exterminate him.

Michael's background in the paranormal field is complex. His mother was an Irish witch, who helped many people during his childhood. Michael inherited some of her abilities. Besides being an experienced investigator, he has the ability to sense and communicate with the spirit world. He walked around my house with his eyebrows raised. I knew he had found something, but he wasn't telling me everything.

"You definitely have something here," he told me. "But, we'll deal with it."

He burned sage, recited prayers, and sprayed holy water on every wall, window, and mirror. He even blessed my pets. He told the entity to leave. All was well for several days.

I got some of my energy back and began feeling like myself again. I felt like I had my life back, until the entity returned. This time would prove to be even worse than the last.

He had me in his sights and he wasn't letting me go. Lucky me.

Chapter 13

In the meantime, life continued like it always does.

Halloween had come and gone. Thanksgiving was weeks behind me. I was so unsettled by the turn of events; I hadn't even taken down my Halloween decorations yet. It would be close to Christmas before I removed the black netting and fake rats from my kitchen window.

I still had to work each day, trying to ignore the feeling that someone was standing right behind me, watching me type. When I was able to make a phone call, I could feel him listening in. The minute I started talking about him, the line would begin to crackle, and I'd soon lose the call.

As disturbing as it was, it made me even more determined to do something about him.

The next fifteen days would be the most terrifying days of my life.

Not only did he follow me throughout my days, he also haunted me at night, whispering in my ear as I tried to sleep. Sometimes he even found his way into my dreams, sending me chilling nightmares of decomposing bodies and bloody sacrifices. I began to believe what the psychic medium told me. He was stronger than a regular ghost and he seemed very intent on collecting my soul.

I could hear his signature sound when he got close to me. I could feel waves of negative energy radiating off him. It was like being in a room with someone who was shouting at me. In that way, he was similar to the grumpy man in the basement of the Victorian, with one exception: I could leave the grumpy man behind, but this one wouldn't allow me out of his sight.

During this time, I was going through some personal issues as well. Thanks to the Soul Collector, I'd been doing pretty well getting over my breakup. I was too busy looking over my shoulder to think about much else, but I had been dreading December first. It was the month that my ex-boyfriend and I planned to go to Florida.

We were going to Orlando to watch his son participate in a Disneyland parade with his high school band. Afterwards, we would spend the week with my father and stepmother in nearby Lake Wales, where they owned a winter home. After the breakup, I changed my ticket date to later in January, but he kept his the same.

I thought about him and our failed relationship that entire week, wondering if he regretted his decision. He had never been a big fan of my ghost hunting, and gave me an ultimatum, saying that I had to quit, or he would leave. Honestly, I didn't think anyone should tell someone else what they *could* or *couldn't* do. I offered a compromise of cutting back to one investigation a month, but he wasn't interested. He made fun of my clairaudient ability, telling me he was worried about me because I thought I had super powers.

I had to roll my eyes at that. If I truly had super powers, I would have shot flames from my eyes, leaving him hairless and crispy.

A week later, one of his family members posted photos on Facebook of his trip to Florida without me. I was heartsick to see that he took another woman in my place. I recognized her from a wedding we attended just before our breakup. I promptly deleted all of his family from Facebook, cried my eyes out, and just tried to move on.

If there's ever been a time in my life when I've been close to a complete emotional breakdown, this was it. I've never been the kind of person to wallow in my sorrows, but this just went beyond anything I was capable of dealing with. I became even more despondent, wanting nothing more than to crawl in a hole, and just stay there until the world was nice to me again.

Thankfully, my friends wouldn't let me hide myself in my pit of despair. Sandy and Tina offered to go back up to Maine with me to visit the psychic medium again. I desperately needed her help.

We met the psychic medium at her house. It was becoming a familiar place.

"I see he's still with you," she said as soon as she opened the door.

I just looked at her and nodded.

She ushered us into her warm family room and offered us drinks. When she came back into the room, I had a question for her.

"What does he look like?" I asked. I wasn't sure if I wanted to know the answer or not, but my imagination was often fairly descriptive. I was hoping that he wasn't as bad as I thought he was.

She told me he was presenting himself as being very tall and thin, with dark hair, and piercing black eyes. She said he reminded her a little of the person in the "Scream" painting, because he liked to open his mouth very wide, as if screaming. And yes, he was still lurking over my shoulder, whispering in my ear, claiming me as his own.

Sandy, Tina, and I exchanged weighted glances. This was just getting worse and worse.

The psychic medium continued. "I think he was a supervisor at the prison. He had a pretty sadistic streak in him," she said with a grim smile. She continued on, telling us that he thoroughly enjoying inflicting pain and humiliation on the inmates under his watch. As she stared into space, trying to pull more information from him, her eyes suddenly grew serious.

"I think he studied dark magick. He did rituals there at the prison," she said.

"What do you mean?" I asked. "Did he do human sacrifices and stuff like that?" My heart was nearly pounding out of my chest.

"I'm not sure if he was able to sacrifice a human or not, but he sure did sacrifice a lot of animals."

"So he worshipped the devil?" I asked.

She studied the air again, narrowing her eyes. "I'd say that's pretty accurate. He was a bad guy. No doubt there."

"What can we do to get rid of him?" I asked, almost afraid to hear the answer.

The psychic medium just shook her head. "He's going to be a tricky one. We'll have to work on him," she told me.

It wasn't the answer I was hoping for. Somewhere in the back of my mind I had hoped she'd had enough time to come up with a good game plan. I was hoping she could finally pull him off of me and spit him back out into the universe. She'd done this for me at Rose Island. The fact that she couldn't easily manipulate this one concerned me greatly.

As our stomachs started growling, we decided to break for lunch. We drove in separate cars to a local diner. While Sandy, Tina, and I followed the psychic medium's car, the ear ringing completely disappeared.

"I don't think your friend is still with us," Sandy said. While her sensitive skills were still developing, there was no mistaking the Soul Collector. Even Tina could feel him, and she wasn't a sensitive. I was elated, until we pulled up at the diner. It returned the minute the psychic medium emerged from her vehicle.

"Well, that was interesting," she told us. "He said that no matter how much praying Charlotte and Mary did; it would never be enough to drive him away."

I was truly shocked. My mother's name is Charlotte and my grandmother, who passed away several years prior, was Mary. The psychic medium had no way of knowing this. It wasn't information I had ever made public. My mother was aware of my situation, but my grandmother was dead. Was she praying for me on the other side?

Then the psychic medium told me something that nearly sent me over the edge.

"Do you have a daughter?" she asked.

"Yes," I answered, feeling my gut clinch appropriately.

She looked down at the ground, clearly dismayed at this information. "I'd try to stay away from her for a little while," she said.

I felt the world literally crumble at my feet. My relationship with my daughter had been strained since my divorce from her father. We were finally starting to make some headway on rebuilding it.

"Why?" I asked, dreading the answer.

"Because he's telling me that if he can't have you, he'll take your daughter instead."

Things just got very bad.

I wasn't sure how I was going to deal with it.

(Below) Joni with her daughter in 1992

(Below) Joni with her daughter and son in Salem 2012

Chapter 14

After my divorce, my daughter surprised me by choosing to live with her father. I always thought the wife got custody of the children. At least that was what I always heard. But, somewhere during the chaos and confusion, my daughter decided that she would rather stay in the town where her friends lived instead of moving to the next town over, where I planned to live.

It actually made sense in the grand scheme of things. As mother and daughter, we were prone to bumping heads. We were both strong-willed women with differing opinions. It was easier for her to get along with her father. This is something I understand, now that time has provided me with some distance.

I've always had an easier time relating to men. Men are easy. If they want something, they'll just tell you. There isn't a hidden agenda, no underlying motives to untangle. What you see is what you get, unless you begin dating one, that is.

Women are a tad different. They have their own hierarchy system. There are rules to follow, agendas to keep track of. You have to look nice, but not too nice. You have to act a certain way, but not come off as if you think you're better than they are. I never really figured them out. After being burned one too many times, I just tried to avoid my gender as much as possible. Tina and Sandy were the first female friends I'd had in years.

After years apart, only seeing each another on occasion, my daughter and I were finally finding a way to reconnect. Things were looking very hopeful. We were both letting go of old resentments that had kept us apart. We were really starting to rebuild our relationship, and it felt wonderful.

I've always been very proud of my daughter. Since birth, she's had a fierce determination. Nothing stands in her way. She just figures out a way to conquer it, and then moves onto the next challenge. I've always been envious, because I've never been this way.

My entire life has been filled with uncertainties. Confidence was something that always eluded me. Was I good enough? Smart enough? Pretty enough? I usually worked towards finding reasons why I wasn't everything I wanted to be instead of trying to make it a reality. I learned a lot from watching my daughter.

She wanted to be an engineer. Without a college fund to draw from, she took out student loans and went away to college, where she would create a very nice future for herself. If she worried about being smart enough, pretty enough, or good enough, she never let it show. She was the beautiful, smart, confident woman I always wanted to be. I was happy for her, and so proud, I could have burst.

She graduated four years later with a mechanical engineering degree. She quickly found a job as a nuclear engineer, making the same yearly salary that I did, after thirty years in the workforce.

So, why didn't I just tell her about it?

As I was writing this, she saw one of my blogs and asked me. I had a hard time answering her. Maybe, it's just something to do with being a mother.

You protect your children from bad things. You keep them as far away from it as possible. You don't introduce them to soul collectors, especially those who have already forewarned you they are interested in your first-born.

The other issue was the theory of ghosts. I hadn't shared a lot of my experiences with my kids. I didn't want to scare them, but more importantly, I also didn't want them to think their mother had gone off the deep end. Talking about ghosts was bad enough, but admitting that I was being stalked by one was quite another. How would I broach this subject without losing the chance to rekindle our relationship?

I probably didn't handle it well. I always try to do the right thing, but there were no instruction manuals on how to proceed through this kind of arena. I postponed our mother-daughter date for that weekend, making up an excuse that probably sounded less than authentic.

I just wanted to keep her safe.

(Below) Tina Aube, Derek Cormier, Joni, Chris Cox, and Sandy MacLeod at the Prison Camp

(Below) Sandy MacLeod and Steven Flaherty at the Prison Camp

Chapter 15

I had to do something now that the Soul Collector was interested in my daughter.

While the psychic medium was very good at giving me insight on who was following me, she was offering very little support on how to get rid of him.

In the aftermath of all of this, people have asked me why someone would provide me with such graphic, chilling accounts of the entity that was stalking me, and then turn me loose without a clear plan for getting rid of it. I don't really have a good answer for this. I think she was trying to help me, but wasn't sure what to do. Other psychics I've spoken with have told me they would never deliberately scare someone with something so horrific until they had a solution. Maybe she was just busy. I knew she was going through some new life choices that affected all aspects of her time and energy, but it still seemed strange.

Over time, I've gotten to know several other psychic mediums. Most of them were born with this ability and have grown used to the lifestyle. Ghosts are just a part of their everyday existence, so they don't get as excited about a spirit attachment. Just push it off, they would tell me.

How?

For me, this ability of sensing ghosts was like driving a car with no steering wheel and no brakes. I was just along for the ride. I tried to do the visualization exercises they recommended. While one recommended sending them off in a boat, another walked me through setting up my own imaginary room, where I could shut off the volume and close the shades. I tried both of the visualization exercises, as well as many others, but couldn't produce any results. As soon as I opened my eyes, everything was exactly the same. My ears were ringing and I could still feel the entity near me.

Most people with my abilities are born with them. By adulthood, they've usually embraced it and have learned how to control it. Even though I was born with this, I spent most of my life pretending it wasn't there. I blamed it on tinnitus. I blamed it on fear itself, convincing myself that getting worked up was causing my ears to ring. I just wouldn't accept it for what it was. When I started ghost hunting, I began tapping into it, using it just like I'd any other piece of equipment, causing it to grow stronger.

My biggest problem was my inability to know what I was dealing with. I felt like a blind women in a room full of people. While I could tell where they were hovering in the room, and even their gender, I didn't know anything else about them. Was he standing there with a butcher knife in his hand, or was he a kindly old grandfather, hoping to pass a message onto his son? I didn't know. They were all the same to me. They were just tones.

After my experience with the Soul Collector, I began assuming they were all knife-wielding demons. It seemed the safest way to be, but it also created a lot of fear I my life. I'd feel one come up to me in a restaurant, and I'd nearly go into a panic, thinking I was going to pick up another bad hitchhiker.

Life became much more difficult once I returned home from Maine. The added knowledge of my spirit attachment did nothing but increase my fear. Before, I would just try to ignore the sensation, but it was impossible now.

Negative entities often feed off heightened emotions. Allowing yourself to be fearful is like giving them a heaping helping of energy. They take it, and then they use it against you. Sometimes I think he tried to scare me on purpose, just to be fed. It was a never-ending circle. I got scared, which just gave him more energy so he could scare me again.

I needed help.

At night, he began touching me more often, his strokes more pronounced than before. I could actually feel him sit down on the side of the bed. First, there was the telltale sound of springs squeaking, followed by the shifting of my covers.

I held my breath, trying to convince myself that it was just my imagination. My heart pounded so loudly, I could feel it in my temples. I wanted to roll over and look, but I was too afraid of what I might find. Would I see an apparition sitting on my bed? I didn't want to find out. I just curled up on my side, with a book propped open in front of me, trying to concentrate on the words, but it was almost impossible.

If I didn't react like he wanted me to, he'd up the ante. He began touching me.

My hair shifted, as though invisible fingers were passing through it. I nearly came unglued. I sat up, searching the room for signs of him.

"Leave me alone!" I hissed into the air.

The room was empty, like it always was. If he was there, he wasn't showing himself.

I eased myself back down on the bed, and tried reading again. The words nearly swam on the page as I tried to focus on them.

Leave me alone. Leave me alone. Leave me alone. I chanted in my mind, praying he'd just listen to me for once.

The respite didn't last for long. After a moment, I felt him touch my hair again. I gritted my teeth, trying not to allow my anxiety to grow, but it was almost impossible. Someone invisible was sitting on the side of my bed touching me. It was all I could do to not run screaming from the room.

His touches grew more pronounced after a while. His hand

moved down the side of my head to stroke my shoulder, before continuing down my body to my hip and leg. It was more than I could take.

"Stop touching me!" I screamed at him.

I could almost hear him chuckling in my head, feeding off this extra helping of fear.

I retreated to the couch in the living room once more.

The next day, I called Sandy and told her about my experience.

"You should try my sleep remedy," she told me. She took two diphenhydramine tablets, along with five milligrams of melatonin. She'd been using it for years, and had great luck with it.

I ran out that morning and picked up a month's supply. The results were heavenly. I could take it a half-hour before bedtime and then escape into sleep. It was my only way to get away from him. If I could ignore the touching and just fall asleep, I was safe. Or so I thought.

Soon, he began finding me there again as well.

I began having more strange dreams. In these dreams, I was lost, and couldn't find my way home. It was always dark there and someone was always chasing me. I woke up several times to see a black shadow run across my bedroom and disappear into my closet. Was it a dream or was it real? I didn't know. I'd find myself out in my hallway, pressing my hands against the closed door, trying to remember how I got there. Had I run out after seeing the shadow figure? Or was it all just a dream? Either way, it was no way to live.

The next morning I called my friend Michael again.

I've since come to think of him as Michael the Exorcist.

Chapter 16

By that time, I had known Michael and his wife Nancy for several years. They were experienced investigators who spent many weekend off investigating the spirit world. We were always hearing about the fantastic locations they went to with their friend, Steven. The three of them often stayed at haunted inns, and traveled to places I always dreamed of visiting. In the years that I knew them, they branched off to start their own paranormal team, and were doing private investigations frequently.

I'd always wanted to do a home investigation, but I wasn't ready. If I couldn't take care of myself and rid myself of unseen entities, how could I possibly help someone else? With my luck, I'd show up, only to bring all of the ghosts back home with me. I couldn't let that happen. I needed to gain better control over my abilities first.

I was curious about Michael's work with the Catholic Church with exorcisms, though.

Exorcisms are the process of expelling demons or other dark entities from either a person or a place where they've claimed ownership. True possession is a terrifying concept. If you've watched enough scary movies on the subject, it's not something you want to have happen to you. In that sense, having a friend who has the inside scoop on such matters seemed like a true blessing.

He'd already been out to my house once to do a house cleansing. I hated calling him again, but I wasn't sure what else to do. Things were becoming so terrifying in my house, and I needed help.

The Soul Collector wasn't keen on the idea.

The minute I picked up my cell phone and started dialing his number, the phone went dead.

The batteries were fine, but the phone shut itself off. After turning it back on, I tried again, only to have the call cut off as soon as it began dialing.

The third time I called, the call went through, but when Michael answered, the line was full of static.

"Sounds like someone doesn't want you to talk to me," he said with a chuckle.

I told him as much as I could before the static became so bad, we couldn't hear each other over it. He promised to come out in a few days.

They showed up with an impressive amount of equipment this time. Over the years, both Michael and Steven have collected various tools of the trade, some of which I'd never even heard of before. We always enjoyed a lesson at investigations, as they demonstrated their newest toys.

They set up a few cameras at various places in the house, and added digital voice recorders, REM pods, and EMF detectors. Steven began snapping pictures with his full spectrum camera, and I was immediately intrigued.

"What does it do?" I asked.

Steven has to be one of the most patient people I know. Ask him anything and he'll stop whatever he's doing to explain it, always adding a humble spin on his response, which makes you feel more comfortable asking. After dealing with many self-professed experts on the subject, it's always refreshing to talk with someone who genuinely cares about sharing his knowledge.

Steven explained how it worked. Typical cameras only provide us with a small range of light. If you look at light on a scale, your normal camera will only capture a small range in the middle. Full spectrum cameras provide you with a broader range with a higher sensitivity, capturing images from ultraviolet to infrared. The theory is clear. A ghost may be visible in a range that a normal camera can't photograph. If you increase the range, you'll have a better chance of capturing it in a picture.

I updated them about my experiences. As I spoke, I could see Michael growing more concerned. He walked around the house, spending time in each room. After a while, he came back with his hands cupped.

"Put your hand between mine and let me know what you feel," he said.

My friends Sandy and Tina had come over to offer emotional support. They were both amazed at what they felt. The air between his hands was much colder than the air around us.

"What is that?" I asked, almost not wanting to learn the answer.

"This is your ghost," he said, smiling.

He couldn't hold onto him for long though. Soon the air between his hands was the same temperature as the air surrounding us. He walked around some more, burning sage and spraying holy water in the shape of a cross over every window, doorway, and mirror.

"This is a tricky one," he said, using the same words to describe it as the psychic medium had.

Normally, when Michael finds something interesting, he emits a deep chuckle that makes the hair on the back of my neck stand up. Hearing a Michael Chuckle is like having every piece of your equipment go off simultaneously. This time he wasn't chuckling though. That was when I realized how serious it was.

Nancy sat at my breakfast bar with her digital recorder, but wasn't having any luck getting a response.

"He doesn't want to talk to us," she said.

"That's because he doesn't want to tell us anything that might help us get him out of here," Michael said.

He gathered his sage, holy water, and his prayers, and spent the better part of an hour working on my house. When he was finished, he was drawn and quiet. The effort had obviously taken a toll on him.

"Okay, he's gone," he said.

I couldn't believe what I was hearing.

"He's really gone?" I asked, looking around me as though I could actually confirm this with my eyes.

Michael nodded, telling me to call him if I had any more problems.

I couldn't believe how easy that was.

The house not only felt lighter, but it looked lighter as well. Gone were the dark shadows and the oppressive mood. Sunshine flooded into the windows, filling the space with the light and love I'd craved to have back in my life. I was so happy, I cried.

I thanked him profusely and watched from my doorstep as everyone drove away.

As I turned back towards my door, I made a mistake that would counteract everything Michael and his friends had just done.

I wondered if it had really worked.

(Below) Michael Cram.

(Below) Nancy & Michael Cram

(Below) The road into the Prison Camp at dusk

(Below) the view from the TB Hospital Ruins

Chapter 17

Doubt can be the undoing of many things. The minute you allow it into your thoughts, you plant a seed of destruction into anything you've attempted. This is especially true in the paranormal world.

Protecting yourself against spirit attachments can be as easy or as difficult as you want to make it. It really hinges on belief. When you believe something will work for you and you hold firm to that thought, it usually works. Unfortunately for me, my inherent skepticism would be my eventual undoing.

Was he really gone?

I walked back into my house with this thought in my mind and then walked around every room, listening. There was nothing at first, but then I started hearing a very faint ringing. It grew louder and louder until he was right back in the room with me.

I must have called him back.

I didn't know what to do.

I couldn't just pack up and move. Every penny I had was tied up in the house, and besides, he would just follow me. I retreated to my sofa again and cried for a long time.

Why me?

After everything I'd already been through, why was this happening to me? When did I get a turn at something good happening to me? I hated falling into a self-depreciating pity party, but once I was in it, I couldn't find my way back out.

I slept on the sofa that night after crying myself to sleep.

The next morning, I woke up stiff and sore. My face was puffy from crying and I was so bone-deep tired, I just wanted to crawl into bed and sleep until it all went away. But, I couldn't even do that. I couldn't walk into my bedroom without feeling his presence so strong I could nearly feel him reaching out to touch me.

I reached out to Michael again.

"He's back," I told him.

Michael was surprised. He saw him leave. He promised to come back, but it would be a few days. In the meantime, I had to live with this negative entity in my house. My friend Sandy gave me several sticks of dragon's blood incense to burn. She said it helps remove negative energy.

I burned a stick, watching the corners of the room, just waiting for something to appear. Nothing was working. Everything we'd tried failed miserably. Was I doomed to live the rest of my life this way? If I got rid of this one somehow, what prevented me from picking up another one? I wasn't sure I could survive that.

The entity made a thump on my headboard, as if laughing at me.

I messaged the psychic medium again with a desperate plea.

"I need help," I told her. I hated sending her message after message. I knew she was going through her own drama, but I had nowhere else to turn.

She responded back quickly this time, promising to help.

I sat in the living room, just staring at the air, waiting for something horrible to happen again, but to my surprise, it felt better. It felt lighter, like after Michael had chased the entity out.

"Oh my God. You did it! He's gone!" I messaged her back.

She told me she'd try to keep him there with her for a while.

I wasn't even sure what to think about this. I had no idea that psychic mediums could pull ghosts from one location and bring them to another. Things like this just didn't happen in my world. At least they hadn't up until that point.

I walked down the long hallway to my bedroom, my heart pounding with fear.

Was he really gone?

Or, was it just a trick?

He was always stronger in my bedroom. Something about that room truly empowered him, allowing him free reign. Unfortunately, it was also my place of refuge. After my divorce and the subsequent series of bad luck events that plagued me over the course of the past five years, I often retreated to my bedroom. That was my crying place. It was the room where I emptied my tears, and then gathered my resolve to try again. It was the place where I went after a long day of work; a place where I could read until I was sleepy, and then fall into a restful sleep. In the course of a few months, it became a place of nightmares.

I walked in and just stood at the foot of my bed, looking around.

Nothing.

I walked to the side of my bed and cautiously sat down.

Still nothing.

I changed into my pajamas and pulled my book off my nightstand. Maybe I'd read for a while and test the waters. An hour later, my eyes grew so heavy; I couldn't keep them open any longer. I started to turn out the light, leaving the room in pitch darkness, like I've always preferred, but I just couldn't do it.

I went into the bathroom and dug around in the closet until I found a nightlight.

I plugged it into the wall and turned it on, happy to have some small measure of light shining in my very dark life.

I fell asleep only to be woken up later by a touch of a hand.

Chapter 18

The days passed as though they were weighted with lead.

Since I worked from home, I seldom left the house. Work had grown much busier and my phone rang incessantly. I was happy for the distraction though. While I answered endless emails and phone calls, my mind was occupied with something other than ghosts.

I was in frequent contact with the psychic medium. She pulled the entity off me as often as she could, but he always found a way to come back. He was like a wayward man, slipping away to his mistress when he had the chance.

"Does he tell you anything when he's there?" I asked her.

She didn't go into details this time, but told me that he wasn't very happy with her. He went back and forth, alternating between berating her from keeping him away from me and then begging her to let him return.

"He says he doesn't mean you any harm one minute, and then the next minute he's telling me he's going to take you whether I want him to or not. He's not good, Joni," she told me.

The torture continued day and night. I'd be busy working, only to hear the familiar sound of him moving into the room behind me. I could feel him standing so close, he was almost touching me. Every cell in my body screamed at me to just bolt, but I couldn't. I had to stand my ground. Besides, where could I run to where he couldn't follow me?

I felt him in the car with me when I drove to the grocery store. He followed me into restaurants when I had the rare chance to eat out. He followed me to friend's houses. It got to a point where I truly expected my friends to start shying away from me.

My friend Tina got a tightening in her chest every time she was around me. It became impossible for friends to spend more than a few minutes inside my house.

"Let's go outside," they'd offer.

I knew it wasn't for the sake of some fresh air or a leisurely cigarette break. It was because they couldn't stand the way my house felt. It was back to being dark and dreary, the energy feeling as depleted as a deflated balloon. The minute I came home, all I wanted to do was to sleep. It was the only place where I could sometimes escape him.

Once again, my friends offered me couches and spare rooms to sleep in, but I couldn't put them in danger too. What would happen if he followed me there and did something horrible to them? I read enough accounts of the supernatural to know that a strong entity was capable of inflicting injuries to people. If he was strong enough to touch me and bang on the walls, then he was probably capable of hurting me or someone else as well.

The psychic medium was quick to calm me. "He won't hurt you. He wants you," she told me. "There's something about you he likes, something he finds attractive."

Awesome. I've never been a pretty girl, but I was attractive enough to often appeal to creepy older men. When I tried a dating site, I was flooded with invitations from men old enough to be my father. Now, I was drawing dead creepers too?

How would I ever bring anyone new into my life with things like this going on? Who would want to sign up for something like that? I could almost see my ad on the dating site: "Single lady with dead people haunting her is looking for a partner." I might as well hang a dead carcass around my neck.

It was almost enough to drag me back into another pity party, but I resisted.

I had a little pep talk with myself.

"You're a survivor. You can handle this," I told myself, taking a deep breath for courage. I had to get through this. There wasn't another option. I've lived most of my life without a safety net. I didn't have any family members a few miles away to offer me an escape. Nobody was going to pay my bills for me if I stayed in bed and refused to deal with it all. If I didn't do it, nobody would. And I had my kids to think about too. My daughter was off at college, but my son still lived with me four days a week. I had to get my life back for both of us.

During this time, I told my son Trevor very little. He'd grown used to the smell of sage. I explained it as a simple house cleansing, a way to improve the energy in the house. He didn't seem affected by it, and I didn't want to scare him needlessly. I would handle this by myself.

The night before Michael returned, something happened to change all that.

The Soul Collector went after my son.

(Below) Joni with her son at his 2013 high school graduation

Chapter 19

I began working on my book again. The literary agent I had been working with for *Lightning Strikes* emailed me back with more changes she wanted me to make. I was determined to transform it into the best book she'd ever read. I wanted her to fall in love with it, breathlessly turning the pages to see what happened next. I dreamed of a book deal, something that would finally launch my dream.

I found myself thinking about the Soul Collector as I wrote. It was impossible not to consider him as he lurked so closely, probably reading over my shoulder. The terror only served to fuel my writing. The agent said that there wasn't enough at stake, that the terrors weren't scary enough for her. I wondered what she would think of the Soul Collector. I wish I could have wrapped him up and shipped him to her with my next manuscript. Instead, I began writing him into the pages.

In the first few drafts of *Lightning Strikes*, the cannibals were just mindless people who wandered the streets. They were a bit like the zombies you see on TV. Thanks to the Soul Collector, I had a brand new appreciation for what "scary" truly looked like. I added a scene in the beginning where a cannibal climbs in Ember's window. As I wrote, the man's face grew long and narrow, his grey hair becoming dark brown. When he looked at her, eyeing her flesh for his next meal, I tapped into those familiar feelings of horror. And it worked. After I read it, I got goose bumps. How could the agent *not* like this? It scared me just reading it and I wrote it!

I was working late one night, sitting at my breakfast bar, just like I am right this moment, typing away on my laptop. I've always dreamed of having a wonderful room where I could retreat to for my writing – and I had it for a while when I was married – but, I made do with what I had. I comforted myself with the thought that one day I'd look back on this, hopefully from the viewpoint of a lavish office, and appreciate it all the more.

The night is darkest before the dawn, I reminded myself.

As I was sitting there musing, it occurred to me that I couldn't hear the Soul Collector's signature tone. I looked around, as if I could actually see him, but nothing was amiss. I often watched the cats when I thought a spirit was in the room. My two old tabbies, Skeeter and Gatorbug, would cock their heads and stare at the ceiling when he was nearby. Both of them were sleeping calmly.

I wouldn't find out the answer until a few minutes later when my son came out of his bedroom.

Trevor often goes to bed much earlier than I do, spending some quiet time reading or watching television, like I was prone to doing. Since I was on such a mission with my book, I was still at my computer when he got up to get a drink of water.

As he came down the hallway towards me, I heard the signature sound of the entity, trailing along behind him. The sound grew stronger as my son came into the kitchen. I tried to act like nothing was wrong, but inside I was in a rage.

How dare he go after my son!

My son got his water and went back into his room, thankfully leaving the evil entity with me in the kitchen. I was so angry I wanted to scream, but I couldn't without my son hearing me. Instead, I spoke in hushed whispers, telling him he'd really crossed a line with me.

"I will stop at nothing to get you out of my house and out of my life," I promised him.

Determined, I turned off my computer and stomped down the hallway to my bedroom.

"And I'm sleeping in my own bed tonight too!" I whispered angrily.

I was so tired of him suppressing me. I was getting mere hours of sleep each night, which was wearing me down a little at a time. By the time Michael and Steve showed up the next day, I was nothing more than a fragment of my former self.

Steven snapped a few pictures with his full-spectrum camera.

"You might wanna take a look at this," he told Michael, after studying one of the digital images on the camera screen.

We passed the camera around quietly, looking at the series of images.

In one photo, a large blob of light, commonly referred to as an "orb" was on my shoulder, right in the place where I imagined him leaning. In the series of shots, the orb could be seen moving down my arm, then finally a distance away from me.

I've never been a believer in orb photos. My opinion is that most orbs are the result of dust or moisture in the air. It reflects in the camera flash, and then shows up on the image as a small circle. What made this one more thought provoking was twofold. Steven didn't use a flash with the photos, so light probably wouldn't be reflected against anything, and the orb was present in several photos, which would be difficult to recreate if it was just a speck of dust or moisture. Also, the path of the orb was traveling out of my body.

"Is that him?" I asked, breathlessly.

"That's him," Michael confirmed.

The orb picture gave me a lot to think about. In my mind, I'd always thought ghosts would look like they appeared before death, in some sort of human form. But in reality, they were nothing more than blobs of energy. I studied the photos some more. Is this what my cats had been watching? Did they see a dot of light moving around the room, very similar to the red dot on their favorite laser toy?

I often saw darts of movement out of the corner of my eye, especially when I was in my bedroom. Was I seeing a small portion of what they were seeing?

I researched it and discovered that a cat's vision is very similar to ours, with the exception that theirs is geared towards detecting motion, something that is useful for them when hunting. They also have a better grasp on colors at the red end of the spectrum, allowing them to differentiate between the hues of blues and violets better than we can. That made some sense, given the photo Steven took with his full-spectrum camera. Were they seeing those orbs move around the room, or were they also hearing the same tones I was hearing?

I learned that cats are able to hear higher pitches than humans can. They can hear up to 64 kHz. That is 1.6 octaves above what humans are able to detect. It's also higher than what a dog can hear, making me wonder even further.

My dog always stayed by my side, even when the activity was at the highest. I've always attributed it to her unwavering devotion, but could it be something more? Was she not hearing the same things my cats and I were hearing? She seldom looked around the room, watching the movements my cats were all actively tracking. She would just put her head down and fall asleep. Sometimes I wondered if that was just her way of dealing with it, something I was doing too.

Michael pulled a small bag out of his pocket and handed me a silver medal. I turned it over, seeing a figure on one side, and writing on the other.

"It's a Saint Benedict medal. I had it blessed by the priest. Put this on and he won't bother you," he told me, showing me the one he had around his neck. "They don't bother me. They don't dare," he said, following it up with his familiar chuckle.

I slipped it on, hoping it was the magic wand I so desperately needed.

The front of the small medal depicts a man standing with his arms out. In his right hand he holds a cross, and in his left hand he holds a book. To his right is a broken cup that was said to have contained poison, and to his left is a raven, who supposedly saved him by carrying away a poisoned loaf of bread. The words "Crux Sancti Patris Benedict" appear above his head, with "Ejus in obitu nostro praesentia muniamus" above it. This translates to "May we at our death be fortified by His presence.

The metal was created in 1880, and was nicknamed "The Jubilee Medal. "People who wear it are supposed to treat it as a visible sign of their inner devotion and belief. By itself, it has no power, but through faith, it is very powerful, providing the wearer with God's blessing and protection through the intercession of St. Benedict.

I slipped it onto a chain almost immediately and latched it around my neck. It was exactly what I needed. It might have just been a piece of metal cast into its current shape, but it was a totem for me to cling to, something to give me hope.

Michael gave some to my friends Tina and Sandy, to keep them safe as well. While he didn't think the Soul Collector would leap to one of them, he wanted them to be careful nonetheless.

He repeated the house cleansing he did earlier, walking around while reciting prayers with a stick of burning sage in one hand and a bottle of holy water in the other. By the time he was finished, the house felt lighter again.

But, then the doubt crept back in.

It had felt lighter the last time too.

"I'm going to do something to help keep you protected," he told me. He took four more St. Benedict medals and buried them at the four corners of my yard. "He won't be able to cross this barrier," he told me. For added security, he also placed one in my basement and another on the door to my attic.

Michael warned me that I had to have faith that this was going to work.

That was hard for me.

Faith was something that I always struggled with. While I truly believed in God and divine intervention, I was skeptical about many of the practices. I was baptized at the age of twelve, at a Congregational Church in Indiana. My religious upbringing involved being dropped off for Sunday school every Sunday when I was a child. I'd fidget through the sermons, paying as little attention as possible. I came to doubt the teachings in the Bible, accrediting them to fables passed down through time.

Some of the stories just seemed too fantastical to be the truth. A man parted the Red Sea? Another man turned water into wine and healed the sick? It seemed like a story that started with a small element of truth, but people exaggerated over time. As the years passed and I tried out various churches, I learned that each religion had its own set of rules as well, deepening my doubt.

One church I went to proclaimed it a sin to dance to music. Another said that drinking alcohol was a way to send you directly to Hell. I saw parishioners hug one another in the confines of the church, only to cut each other off in the parking lot. Was this what I wanted, what I wanted to believe in?

I came to form my own opinions about religion. For me, it was about being a good person. It was a matter of always trying to do the right thing, especially when it came to people. I followed the Golden Rule and treated others as I wanted to be treated. I went out of my way to make people feel good about themselves. After years of being bullied as a child, this wasn't a hard concept to grasp. My church wasn't confined to the inside of a building. I carried it around with me everywhere I went.

Wearing a medal of a man who had been blessed by the eyes of the Catholic Church didn't carry much merit with me. Who was this man, really? And, more importantly, did he really do the things they said he did, or was this just another tale passed down through the ages?

I liked the concept of having something to latch onto for protection, but I would always question it. It would swiftly undo the protection that Michael had so carefully constructed.

They left, telling me to call them if I needed them. As I watched them leave, I got that sinking feeling in my stomach again.

How long this time? How long before he returned?

(Below) Joni wearing her St. Benedict's Medal
in her *Lightning Strikes* author photo

Chapter 20

I've never been a superstitious person. I have a black cat that crosses my path at least a hundred times a day. I've broken mirrors without having any measurable amount of bad luck, and I've walked under ladders with no ill effects.

So, what was the difference between superstition and religion?

It was a deeper topic, and I wasn't sure how I felt about it. Was holding onto a St. Benedict medal any different from holding onto a lucky rabbit's foot or four-leaf clover? Was it the simple belief that made the difference?

Some people think that protecting yourself against paranormal attachments involves your level of belief. If you believed without a shadow of doubt that nothing could attach to you, then it couldn't. Once you introduced doubt, it shattered at your feet, as useless as an umbrella full of holes.

I do think there's some merit to this. Scientists say we only utilize a small portion of the brain. Is it possible that those of us with psychic abilities are simply tapping into a part of our brain that others are not using? Is there another part of the brain that helps us prevent spirit attachment?

I began wondering what I was missing. One of my friends, who is a powerful energy worker, set up a class for me and Sandy. He said that if we worked on manipulating our energy, we could force the spirits to stay away from us.

Sandy seemed to grasp onto it faster than I did. She has amazing energy. After the lesson, she learned to create an invisible shield of energy around herself, and then would push the energy outward, moving entities out of her personal space. I didn't have as much success with it.

I went home, eager to try this with the Soul Collector, but it didn't seem to have any effect. I could push all I wanted, but he wouldn't budge.

Maybe he was just a stronger entity. Through all of this I've started compiling my own belief system of the supernatural. I think that when people die they are supposed to cross over into the white light. When they do, they move to another realm of existence, a place where they review their life on Earth, and then make decisions on where they will go for their next life.

Does this mean I believe in reincarnation?

Probably. I can honestly say that I believe in a lot of things that I used to scoff at, but my belief is as translucent as my faith. There's just so much we don't know. I wouldn't be willing to stake my life on anything at this point.

So, what happens when people don't cross into the light?

I think they become earthbound ghosts. They hang around for a variety of reasons. Some stay because they have unfinished business, such as a loved one they want to look after, or a task they didn't complete. Others who died suddenly, or even by their own hand, might not even realize they are dead. They abruptly find themselves floating around without a body, unable to do much more than witness what is going on in our world. Learning to communicate with the living is something they must practice and develop over time.

I also believe the longer they stay in ghost form, the more they begin to forget about their former lives. It's as though they lose touch with their human origins, becoming something totally different. This would explain why we seldom received clear intelligent responses. In losing their physical bodies, do they also lose their logic and reason? Unfortunately, the questions only bred more questions.

Before Michael left, he warned me about something that

made me very uneasy. He spoke about the three levels of demonic possession. He counted them off on his fingers: infestation, oppression, and possession.

By my own observations, if this was a true demon haunting, then I had moved well beyond the first phase. I was deeply embedded in the second.

Oppression had become a way of life for me.

What was next?

(Below) Joni's house after the freak Halloween blizzard

Chapter 21

Michael wasn't gone very long before I felt the entity return.

I found myself going from hopeful to hopeless in a matter of hours. My ears began ringing again, and I could feel him hovering behind me. Things in my house began disappearing, and then reappearing somewhere else. At first, I blamed it on my sleep-deprived mind, but then I came to realize that it was all interconnected.

He was getting to me.

I'd find myself simply phasing out. At a group party, I just sat in a lawn chair staring into space until someone shook me out of it. I didn't feel like myself. I felt like I was missing huge gaps of time. I'd find myself looking at the clock, dismayed to discover that hours had passed, instead of minutes. Where was I during this time? This spirit seemed stronger than a regular entity. Something wasn't quite right.

I called the psychic medium again.

"It seems much stronger than a regular spirit. What do you think it is?" I asked her, almost too afraid to hear the answer.

What she told me was hard to believe.

"You know I told you that I thought he practiced dark magick at the Prison Camp?" she asked

"Yes," I said, hesitantly.

"Well, I think that whatever he called attached itself to him."

"What do you mean?" I asked, my heart racing at the mere thought of a demon being involved.

"I think that he is more than just a negative entity. I think he might have started out human, but when he died, the demon took over."

I clutched the phone to my ear.

"He's a demon?" I asked.

"He might be," she said.

I had a lot to think about after I hung up the phone. I am a logical person by nature. I never had my fortune told, nor did I give much thought to horoscopes or astrological charts. I've always had to prove things to myself before I fully believed them.

Ghosts were easy for me to believe in because I had proof of their existence. I'd been on investigations and captured EVPs. On two occasions, I actually witnessed the appearance of a full body apparition. I had the proof that I needed to solidify my beliefs, but demons? Was there really such a thing?

Before I could believe in demons, I had to believe in angels. Heaven and Hell weren't far behind. Could I even grasp onto this concept?

The thought of demons truly terrified me. If I looked at case studies and read about other people who'd had demonic experiences, I had to give it some weight. It seemed like there might be something out there that was more powerful than a negative entity.

Many paranormal researchers don't believe in demons. They feel that, just like in life, there are good spirits and there are bad spirits. They think that when we die, we take that inherent goodness or badness with us to the other side. The truth is: nobody really knows for sure.

By classification, demons are non-human entities. Their entire purpose is to destroy humans. Nearly every culture believes in them. They are malevolent, evil entities and they are always hungry for a soul to possess.

I'd seen enough movies to form an opinion on them. I'd never seen one before, but was open to the idea. But, was it happening to me? Really?

It really seemed far-fetched.

My paranormal friends get frustrated with me at times because of my skeptical nature. On investigations, I'm always looking for a logical answer. I'm usually not impressed with orb photographs, or faces that seem to appear in windows. I blame a lot of this on matrixing. The human brain is programmed to look for faces. We see something that looks like two eyes and a mouth, and if we allow it, it looks like a face, but if we look closer, we'll see that it's really nothing more than the reflection of the shrubbery, or a smudge of dirt on the window. When a door closes by itself, I play with it, trying to see if something in the mechanics is causing it to close.

Buying into my paranormal experiences truly took a leap of faith for me, something I wasn't easily prone to giving into. If I couldn't see it with my own eyes, hear it with my own ears, or experience it personally, I would always be doubtful.

While I could grasp the concept of ghosts, demons were much more of a stretch, but I was willing to entertain the possibility, but a ghost with a demon attachment? It wasn't something I was going to tell my mother about.

Sometimes I wondered if I was just losing my mind.

What if the ear ringing was just tinnitus?

What if the feelings that someone was lurking close was just my imagination?

What if the thumps on the walls were just the house settling?

What if my cats were just watching shadows?

As I thought about it, I had to circle back around and look at it as a whole. If one of these things were happening, I could easily explain it, but the fact that all of them were happening made it hard to ignore.

It was really happening.

Whether it was a demon, or simply a negative spirit, it was real, and it had its sights set on me.

God help me.

(Below) Joni's bedroom

Chapter 22

The psychic medium told me she would perform a protective spell for me. It eased my mind a little. Besides being a very talented psychic medium, she was also a second-generation witch, someone you would never want to cross, but also someone you wanted on your side when something like this came up.

I knew very little about witches and what they could do, but I respected them nonetheless. I'd seen some very strange things by this point and I wasn't counting anything out.

I began to read about witches, learning that they were far different than I had imagined.

I think when most people hear the word "witch" they get a mental image in their head that probably coincides with Halloween; however, what I learned couldn't have been further from the truth. Witches in general are a very peaceful, Earth-loving group.

They believe in magick, and casting spells as part of rituals. Most witches only cast spells for good purposes. The philosophy is that anything that is sent out will return to you three-fold. Cast a negative spell against someone, and you'll get it back three times worse.

As I've gotten to know several witches, I've learned that practices and beliefs vary from witch to witch. While most witches are true Pagans, some also believe in the same God the Christian faith worships. Some practice spells for good purposes only, while others sometimes cast spells of a darker nature. They are all individuals with varied practices.

If I had any doubts about spell casting, they were quickly erased once the psychic medium performed the protection spell. He'd been looming close to me all day and then suddenly he was simply gone.

I quickly messaged her. "He's gone!" I told her.

"Good, it worked," she responded.

It lasted right up until bedtime.

I walked into my room, feeling a hopefulness I hadn't felt in a long while. Maybe I could actually go back to my old life. I could lie in bed, read for a while, and then fall off into a dreamless slumber. The minute my head hit the pillow, I felt him return.

It was like getting a Christmas present, only to have it whisked away.

I messaged the psychic medium again, and she promised to try it again.

I knew she was getting tired of my constant requests. While she was always pleasant and did what she could, I still felt bad always reaching out to her. She had a life of her own, with her own troubles to deal with. The last thing she needed was a needy ghost hunter constantly begging for help.

If I could have done it myself, I would have. I just didn't know how.

I spent the next two nights doping myself up with my sleep remedy. If I was lucky, I could wait until my eyes were heavy with sleep, and then launched myself into my bed to fall directly asleep. If I were really lucky, I'd sleep all the way through the night without being woken up.

Most nights this didn't happen.

The psychic medium told me that since the protection spell didn't work, she would do a banishing ritual for me.

I'd never heard of such a thing and was too frightened to ask what it entailed. She assured me that she could do it without a need for me to be present. Her coven would handle it, but they had to wait until the time was right.

Dear God, what was happening to me?

As scared as I was, I probably would have been even more frightened if I hadn't already had other experiences with the paranormal.

My first paranormal experience happened when I was seven years old.

I woke up from a dream that I'd been having every single night for a week.

In the dream, I was on a chairlift, heading up a steep hill beside an old wooden barn. Someone was whispering in my ear the entire way up, demanding that I made a choice. He said that if I didn't sacrifice myself to him, he would take every member of my family, starting with my younger sister, Leah. I woke up to find myself staring at my doorway.

In the doorway, a misty white shape lingered. As I watched, it floated slowly in my direction, not stopping until it reached my bed.

I was awake. I know it wasn't part of my dream, because I could feel every texture of the moment. My sheets were tangled around my legs, and my nightgown was wet with perspiration. As the entity grew closer, I could feel the anger and ill intent washing off him in waves. He came all the way to the side of my bed, mere inches away from me and just stood there.

I finally found my voice and screamed for my mother.

He dissipated as my mother raced down the hallway towards me, but I could still feel him lingering. For the next months, I'd feel him visit me on a nightly basis as I hid beneath the covers, terrified.

I started sleepwalking shortly afterwards.

My parents would wake up to hear my screams, as I tore through the house. Nothing would wake me up. They shook me, tried to carry me back to bed, and even threw water in my face, but I remained firmly in my sleep state. When I finally came out of it, I would look around, not remembering any of it, except for the dream that wrapped its tentacles around me, pulling me throughout the house.

I was no longer allowed to watch anything even remotely scary on television, including my favorite show, *Scooby Doo*. They even took away all of my *Nancy Drew* books. After several months, things seemed to go back to normal, or at least that's what they thought. I stopped talking about things I was seeing at night, during my sleepwalks. I began waking up on my own.

I still sleepwalk to this day. Sometimes, I'll wake up in the strangest places. Once I woke up sitting on my bathroom sink with my face inches away from the mirror, staring deeply into my own eyes. When I was married, my husband would try to tackle me to stop me from bolting, but that usually only resulted in bruises and unnecessary injuries. When I walk in my sleep, I do so with my eyes wide open. I'm sure this must have been a creepy experience for anyone experiencing it, especially the roommate I had on a yearly meeting for work. I woke up with her asking me what the hell I was doing. I found myself bent over her, slapping the headboard on her bed.

"I was trying to turn off the bomb, of course," I told her and then walked calmly back to bed. Thankfully, I'd warned her the night before that I was prone to nightly walks.

My daughter went through this as a child, as well. At the time, we called them "night terrors," but it bothered me to watch her following in my footsteps. After learning that the Soul Collector was interested in her, it made me wonder if we shared anything else.

Unfortunately, this experience in my youth wouldn't be the last paranormal experience I would have.

There were several others.

Below) One of Joni's cats, watching movement in the room

Chapter 23

When I was pregnant with my daughter, we purchased our first house. It wasn't anything fancy, just a small blue ranch on a quiet street in the town of Westborough, Massachusetts. Nothing seemed amiss when we first moved in. We were eager to carve out a space for ourselves and immediately started renovating.

It had two small bedrooms, a living room, one bathroom, and a kitchen. It was just the right size for a young family with a child on the way. I walked around the rooms, blissfully happy to have a home of our own. Little did I know what awaited me.

The only part of the house that I didn't like was the basement. It was appropriately spooky, with dirty cement walls, and cobwebs hanging from the ceiling rafters. It was apparent the former owners used the room often. The wall behind the fireplace was painted a deep blood-red, and a giant workbench covered another wall. It was the sort of workbench you could imagine being used frequently over the course of several decades. It was scarred and worn and had settled in against the wall, like an appendage.

Nothing happened in the house until we tore the workbench out and began turning the room into a family room. Then the activity started.

It started slowly, with small incidents. A tool would disappear, only to be discovered in another location. We attributed it to the dogs at first, but then it began happening while the dogs were locked away in their crates. We just scratched our heads.

I had believed in ghosts since my childhood experiences, but I couldn't imagine something like this happening to us in our new home. The former resident lived there for seven years and prior to that, an older couple lived there even longer.

Several years went by and the little things started adding up. Was our house haunted?

We weren't sure, but it wasn't anything we really fixated on. We just turned a blind eye on it, hoping that if we didn't acknowledge it, it would just go away.

But, it didn't.

Soon the activity escalated. We started hearing footsteps. Our daughter was only a baby and no one else was in the house when we first heard them. It sounded as though someone was walking across the living room floor above us. We raced upstairs, only to find the room empty.

Someone was obviously trying to get our attention.

But, who?

It came to a point where we had to actually deal with it. It was clear that it wasn't going away, but what could we do? This happened long before any paranormal shows were on television and the Internet was still in its infancy, offering slow dial-up service and a pay-by-the-minute usage plan, so information wasn't even readily available. I went to my local library and began reading as much as I could on the subject. What I found was sparse and outdated.

I was embarrassed to mention it to friends and family, because I was fearful that they'd think I was crazy. As it turns out, the ghost would let them know on his own.

My sister-in-law often babysat my daughter. She would pick her up from daycare, and then bring her to our house until we came home from work. We didn't tell her about the haunting, but she soon found out. On more than one occasion, she showed up at our house, only to find the doors open and the all the lights on. Sometimes the dogs would be let out of their crate.

The house began developing a heaviness. It made our chests

tighten the minute we walked in the door. Unseen eyes glared at us as the presence followed us around the house. We began to wonder out loud about what was happening, naming the unseen entity, "Gus," after a children's book character.

At the time, I was very young and uncertain about anything paranormal. All I had to compare my experience with were the horrific movies on television and my own limited experiences. Was it a poltergeist? Was our house built on old gravesites? Should we just move out?

I was attempting to write my first book at the time, a horror novel about an escaped serial killer who was stalking a woman. It probably wasn't the best book to write, given our current situation, but it was strong in my head and I needed to get it out on paper.

I worked on the book every chance I got, but with a toddler at home, time was often difficult to find. I stayed up late, writing while everyone in the house slept, getting a page or two completed a day. This was back in the days before everyone had home computers, so I wrote on a word processor that stored the writing on small grey disks. As we left for dinner one night, I began looking for the disk where I'd stored the book. I had set it right on the bar in the basement, which was located in the same spot the old workbench once resided, but it was nowhere to be found. When we returned later, I walked to the bar again, just for one more look, and there it was, right where I'd left it.

We went through all the logical assumptions. Someone must have broken into the house and moved it. Both of us had looked for it and knew darned well it wasn't on the counter when we left. Who though?

We wouldn't understand that our jokes about Gus were real until the writing appeared on the wall.

I was a big tropical fish enthusiast back then, so my husband built an aquarium inside a wall for me in the basement, with access inside a closet so I could clean it. I left on a trip to Indiana to visit my family, and when I returned, he proudly showed me the aquarium. I walked inside the closet to see what it looked like from the other side, and stopped dead in my tracks.

In between two studs on the backside of the paneling, someone had written something in chalk.

I'm here woman.

The letters were shaky, but were undeniably there. Even the apostrophe was in place. Was this message for me, being the only woman in the house? Why was he telling me this?

My ears began ringing, softly at first, then more urgently. I began getting the sensation that someone was watching me. Instead of staying up late to write, I soon I found myself running up to bed behind everyone else. There was no way I was going to be downstairs alone.

After we'd been in the house for six years, and had expanded our family with the birth of my son, we built a second floor onto the house. This only seemed to offend Gus even more. Doors slammed on their own accord, toilets flushed all by themselves, and strange sounds could be heard in the house. There was no longer a safe place to hide. The house was active, even during the daylight hours. It got to a point where I began spending as much time outdoors as possible, walking my son to a nearby playground or playing in the yard with him while my daughter was at kindergarten.

My daughter eventually outgrew her night terrors, but that didn't mean she was left out of the activity. When she was seven, we both witnessed a dark shadow race past the basement window. As soon as it ran by, the door opened with a blast of wintery air. I ran to close it, locking it tight, terrified at what was happening.

I endured this for thirteen long years. When my husband

suggested we sell the house and move further into the country, I was elated to leave. Unfortunately, Gus had other ideas. People who came to look at the house always ended up walking out with their eyebrows drawn. It took nearly a year to find someone willing to live there.

I later learned that the house was sold five times in the next five years.

We'd apparently woken something up.

It would be another ten years before I would experience something as frightening, only this time I did it alone. When I went to bed, I had no one there to comfort me.

It was just my cats and me.

My cats eventually bolted from the room, with their ears flattened.

I wasn't sure what to do.

It was slowly killing me.

(Below) The house in Westborough

Chapter 24

December was a solemn month for me. With my family a thousand miles away, I was facing Christmas alone. Gone was the promise of a forever relationship. Gone was all my hope and good cheer. I stared at the box of Christmas decorations for several weeks before forcing myself to make an effort.

This wasn't where I expected to be at forty-seven. I thought I'd be married with my nearly-grown children popping in and out of the house, keeping me busy with their activities. I'd live in a big house and take a nice family vacation every year. Instead, I was here. Alone.

I put up a small tree, and then hung a few decorations around the house, hoping it would cheer me up, but all it did was to remind me of what I'd lost, and also what I was dealing with. My house felt more like Halloween than Christmas, and I just wasn't in the mood to deal with it.

My health was beginning to have an effect on me. The lack of sleep and constant stress led to frequent chest pains and migraines. I got to a point where I just didn't care. I just stretched out on the couch, mindlessly staring at the television set. My cats would come to greet me and I began to wonder who would take care of them when I was gone.

It was clear to me that my life was over. Everything was coming to a head. There was no way I was going to survive this, any of it. Then I got news that nearly sent me right over the edge.

The literary agent I'd been working with for nearly a year on my book, *Lightning Strikes*, told me she wasn't going to represent me. She felt the book lacked the right pacing and didn't follow the dystopian format, like she wanted. I was back to square one.

I couldn't imagine putting this book in a box in my closet. I was all out of do-overs. I didn't have the strength to start another book that would probably end up in the closet with the others. I began to give up on my dream, and in doing so, I began to give up on life itself.

I began to daydream about how I was going to do it. I found myself drifting towards large trees, my foot planted firmly on the gas. I began to wonder exactly how many sleeping pills it would take. The only thing that stopped me was the thought of my children.

How could I leave them like this?

If I went through with this, I'd never get to see my children graduate from college or hold my first grandchild. I'd be a faded memory by the time they were adults, someone who ruined their childhood with her own selfish needs. I was stuck in a very bad place.

One cold December morning, I woke up to two things that saved me.

One was an email from the psychic medium. She had finally arranged for the banishing ritual she'd been telling me about. The other was a call from my friend, Michael.

"Are you okay? Just checking on you," he said.

From the tone of my voice, he knew I was far from okay. He promised to come out to my house the next day for another cleansing ritual.

Things happened very quickly at that point, and I'm glad.

If they didn't, I might not have survived them.

Chapter 25

When Michael showed up with Nancy and Steven, he wasn't his normal chipper self. He was concerned. He finally told me what I was dealing with.

"It's not just a ghost. It's a demon," he told me.

I shivered at the thought. In a way, he was confirming what the psychic medium told me. Hearing it from two different sources that were completely separate from each other, was appropriately terrifying.

Demons were something you saw on TV and in movies, not something that bothered with ordinary people like me. It was simply beyond comprehension.

He had previously told me that the three stages of a demonic possession were infestation, oppression, and finally possession.

"You're in oppression," he told me. "We need to do something about this now before it's too late."

He brought a book this time and began reading prayers from it. He walked around the house with burning sage and his bottle of holy water, spraying it on every wall, window and doorway of my house. As he went along, I began to grasp what the prayers were about.

"Are you doing an exorcism?" I asked.

He wouldn't confirm this, because he was a layman, not a member of the clergy. He said if this didn't work, he would contact the Catholic Church to get approval for an exorcism. But, he was reading some of the same prayers.

Thoughts swirled in my head. An exorcism? Was this really happening?

In my heart, I'm still just an Indiana farm girl, the kind of person who would never end up going through something like this. What did I do to bring something like this on myself?

After he was finished, the house seemed quieter, but as I went into my bedroom, things took a turn for the worse.

It turned out the Soul Collector still had one more trick up his sleeve.

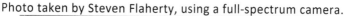

(Below) Michael Cram blessing Joni's house. You can see the anomaly on Joni's shoulder.
Photo taken by Steven Flaherty, using a full-spectrum camera.

Chapter 26

Michael, Nancy and Steven left, satisfied they'd chased the demon out of my house.

As Michael got into his car, he told me to call him if anything else happened. He had already contacted a priest, and would work with the church to get permission to do an exorcism if needed.

I walked back inside, my heart heavy with emotion.

What if it didn't work? What if even the exorcism wasn't successful? What would happen to me? I could already see the effects it was having on my health and well-being. There was hardly anything left of me at that point. All my fight was gone. I just wanted to hide until it all went away.

I took my book and put it in the closet with the others and I retreated to the couch.

My son came home later in the evening and I tried to put on a happy face for him. The last thing I wanted was for him to be afraid. A part of me wanted to warn him about it, but the other part was afraid of the ramifications. Negative energies feed on fear. If I brought him into my private little horror show, what would it do to him? Would the entity begin targeting him as well?

I just wanted it all to end.

I messaged the psychic medium again, asking about the banishing ritual. She quickly confirmed that they still planned to hold it at ten o'clock that night.

After my son went to bed, I went into my bedroom.

My ears began ringing almost immediately with his signature sound.

"Why won't you just go away?" I pleaded with him, tears streaming down my face.

The room was silent.

I sat on my bed and leaned against the headboard, just looking around the room. So much of what I was experiencing was invisible. I could hear his tone, feel him literally hanging over my shoulder, anger radiating off him in waves.

Was I just crazy?

I'd been down this road many times. If I were crazy, would everyone else be picking up on it as well? Would my cats flatten their ears as they stared at the ceiling before bolting from my bedroom? Would I be hearing all the bangs on the walls? One thing was for certain, I wasn't going to tell anyone about it. I was going to keep it to myself.

But then I began thinking about it. So many people get into ghost hunting because it sounds fun and exciting. They wander into haunted locations, hoping for an experience, just like I did, never considering the effects it could have on them.

While ghosts don't follow most people, they do sometimes follow sensitives. I didn't realize I was a sensitive, in the truest sense of the word, until I was in my late thirties. How many other people have some sort of ability they haven't come to terms with yet? Would they also find out the hard way, as I did? Maybe one day I would tell my story, but I had to survive it first.

By nine-thirty, I was nearly beside myself with worry. I imagined the witches gathered around the altar, lighting candles to prepare for the ritual. The psychic medium had reached out to several other witches in other covens, as well. They planned to do similar rituals at their own altars. "This will work," she told me.

Most of what I experienced was invisible, but he had one more trick up his sleeve before the ritual began.

I saw a shaft of light appear near my bedroom doorway. It was about three feet long and hovered in the air like magic. As I watched, it tilted to the side, and then began bouncing around the room as if on an invisible string.

I wanted to bolt from my room, but I took a deep breath instead.

Fear only feeds him.

"That's what he wants," I told myself. "He's trying to build energy to fight the ritual. Just stay calm."

The rod of light disappeared soon after, and I just sat there, watching the clock, my ears ringing so loudly, it nearly split my skull.

I could feel him trying to get to me. Words began appearing in my mind.

Just let me stay. I won't hurt you.

Chills ran down my spine.

"You have to go," I told him.

What your friends are doing won't work with me. I'm too strong.

"I don't believe you," I said. I already knew that doubt was not my friend. I had to believe what they were doing was working. My entire life depended on it.

Even though he was still pulling his tricks, he felt a little weaker. I had to wonder if Michael Cram's efforts had weakened him. If they had, it might give the witches a better chance to remove him.

At ten o'clock, I just sat stock-still on my bed.

It was finally happening.

I erased all doubts, not wondering if it would work or not.

It WOULD work.

It had to.

At ten fifteen, I began to hear his signature sound fade away. It receded into the distance, and then disappeared completely with a pop.

He was finally gone.

Chapter 27

I fell into a dreamless sleep, the kind I was denied for months. When I awoke the next morning, my entire world was different.

The sun shone brightly through the blinds, painting stripes across my bed where my two cats lounged.

"My big, brave kitties," I crooned to them, enjoying the sound of their purrs as I petted them.

I didn't blame them for being fearful. It was more than most humans could handle. I couldn't imagine what they must have been going through as they lived through my nightmare. Having them back in my room, purring on my bed, was a good sign though, and I was happy to see it.

Mindful that it was a workday, I pulled myself out of bed and began getting ready for my day. Since I worked from home, my commute to my home office was only a matter of a few steps. I logged onto my work computer, happy to hear nothing more than the whir of the fan.

My ears were no longer ringing. I could have jumped for joy.

I called the psychic medium later in the morning.

"How did it go?" I asked.

"He's gone, isn't he?" she said with a laugh. "He was a real bugger though."

She went on to tell me that he was very resistant, literally begging them to stop as they neared the end. She said that he eventually just ceased to exist.

"Where did he go?" I asked, my heart starting to pound once more.

"He just went away, like a candle being blown out," she told me. I thought about the way I'd heard the sound of him fading away, followed by the sound of a pop. That must have been when they removed him from our world.

I spoke to another member of the coven later and she filled me in with more details.

Jennifer Julian is a practicing witch with historic roots. Her eighth great-grandmother and one of her grandmother's sisters were killed during the Salem witch trials. Mary Eastey was the grandmother, and Rebecca Nurse was her sister. While Jennifer isn't certain if Mary and Rebecca were truly witches or not, she does know she inherited the ability from someone.

Drawn to the Pagan religion, she would find herself frequently crossing paths with other witches who would play a role in her life. She'd become fast friends with these women, each of them teaching her valuable lessons before making a timely exit.

She had spoken at great length with the psychic medium about how they would get rid of the Soul Collector. They had a new member in their coven and they worried about involving her. In the end, they decided that they truly needed her energy if they were going to pull it off.

"She knew the risks and wanted to help," Jennifer said.

Jennifer was always the one to open and close their circles.

"That night I was extremely focused on the task at hand. I just knew what we were doing had to work," she said.

She always envisioned a whitish-purplish energy surrounding them as she cast her circles, often doubting they were cast correctly. This time she had no doubt. They could all feel the energy. It was stronger than anything they'd ever experienced.

"We discussed the fact that the three of us were meant to be doing what we were doing," she said. Apparently, someone was looking out for me after all. All the pieces were now in place.

The psychic medium wrote a banishment spell that they used, along with a male figure candle that was black. They appointed the candle with various herbs and oils, and then wrapped it in muslin to bind the malevolent spirit to the candle. Once it was completed, they all knew the spell worked successfully. They felt him leave, just like I had.

They decided together to leave the circle open for protection through the night just in case, knowing that the energy would eventually dissipate on its own.

When I spoke with the psychic medium the following morning, she was apprehensive about telling me the rest. What she told me will remain with me for the rest of my life.

"I have to tell you something and it might freak you out a little, but after the ritual, we blew out all the candles and went upstairs. A half hour later, the smoke detector in the basement started going off. We went down to look and the alter cloth was all burnt up."

The ashes spelled out three letters. L-E-O.

My friend Michael would later tell me that it was probably trying to spell out Legion, something referenced in the Bible, referring to a group of demons who roamed the earth.

We are legion.

I was then told to wipe the last six months from my mind.

Don't think about him.

Don't talk about him.

And, whatever you do, don't write about him.

If you do, he might come back.

I've never been very good at taking directions.

I needed to get my story out, in case it could help someone else.

So far, so good, but that doesn't mean I'm not watching the shadows for movement.

Please keep me in your prayers, because I might need it.

The Aftermath

My life began to turn around almost immediately.

Gone were the oppressive thoughts, the terror of walking into my own bedroom, the thought of ending my life just to escape from his grasp. In its place grew a small sprig of hope.

I began dating again, after meeting a nice man on a dating site. The relationship wouldn't last the winter, but it was a starting place. I needed to learn how to live again, and it started with getting out of my house.

My friends Sandy and Tina rallied around me, introducing me to Marion Luoma, who would soon become another close friend. We held off on the ghost hunting for a while though. While it had always been a favorite past time of ours, I no longer felt the need to poke at things I couldn't see. I still go on the occasional investigation, but most of what I do is geared towards assisting or educating others. I help Sandy with her meet-up group, teaching others important lessons on how to protect themselves and how to conduct a respectful investigation. I also only go to places I trust.

As for my book? I didn't give up on that either.

One of my friends suggested I look into self-publishing my book instead of leaving it in the closet. I pulled it out, dusted it off and gave it a fresh dose of hope.

I released it a month later to astounding reviews. Six months later, I would release the second book in the trilogy, adding the third installment just four months after that. Readers praised the books. Nearly every reviewer mentioned how fast-paced the books were, and pointed out how they couldn't stop reading them once they got started. If they only knew what I was going through when I wrote them, I thought with a smile.

In reality, I am still a skeptic. I will always be a skeptic. I can't say for certain this was indeed a demonic attachment, but I can say that it happened to me. This isn't *based* on a true story. It *is* a true story. Being a writer with an excellent imagination, I could have easily embellished my story, but I didn't. I wanted to tell it exactly like it happened.

All in all, it changed the way I look at the world.

I began to believe in destiny and fate. I started viewing my life as a series of challenges and opportunities, steps on a path that would lead me to the place where I'm supposed to be. If my boyfriend hadn't broken up with me, I never would have gone onto to write my trilogy, nor would I have founded such deep friendships with the people who stood by me in my time of need.

Life would go on.

Nothing bad would happen to me for another year, not until I returned to the Prison Camp to face my fears.

The next one I picked up wouldn't prove to be as bad as the first. I was also better prepared to handle with it.

I've come to learn that I am a beacon. Spirits are attracted to me. I've just learned to deal with it. It's just a part of my world now, something I will live with for the rest of my life.

It's a very strange life, but it's *my life* all the same.

I'm planning to make the best of it.

No matter what it takes.

(Below) My Angels of Ember trilogy! Available on Amazon.com for Kindle and in paperback format.

(Below) My very first book signing at Barnes and Nobel's Book Store in Evansville Indiana on 6/15/13. It was an amazing feeling, sitting at that table, especially after all I'd gone through.

Protecting Yourself During an Investigation

The methods of protecting yourself during an investigation are varied and diverse. Here are several of the more common practices.

Before the Investigation

1. **State of Mind** - Always be in a good state of mind. If you are depressed, tired, or just not in a good place, don't go. With your resistance down, you are more susceptible to spirit attachment.

2. **Prayer** – There are many to choose from and this works for many people. If you don't follow any faith or have a spirit guide, then use the time to tell yourself you will be safe, and that you will be protected.

   I prefer the St. Michael's Prayer, as follows:
   Saint Michael the Archangel,
   defend us in battle;
   be our protection against the wickedness and snares of the devil.
   May God rebuke him, we humbly pray:
   and do thou, O Prince of the heavenly host,
   by the power of God,
   thrust into hell Satan and all the evil spirits
   who prowl about the world seeking the ruin of souls.
   Amen.

3. **Medallions or Religious Symbols** – Any medallion that makes you feel safe will help with your protection. I have a rose quartz necklace Sandy made for me. I wear it all the time, because it was made with good intent and it makes me feel protected. You can wear a cross/crucifix, a saint medallion, a wiccan star pentagram, a crystal or a Celtic symbol: whatever holds your belief system, and you feel comfortable while wearing it.

4. **Protection Spray** – Containing essential oils and fragrances, this can help ward off negative energy. It is readily available from many different sellers online. Remember the smell as you investigate, and don't mistake it as a sign from the spirits.

5. **Sage** – Often referred to as "smudging,", the burning of sage began as a Native American ritual for cleansing and blessing people and places. It changes the energy, altering the vibration level, and leaves the space in better harmony. White sage is best and can be mixed with sweet grass or cedar. While burning the sage, take turns allowing the smoke to cover each other completely. Start with the bottom of your feet, working upwards, making sure to cover the front and the back of the person. When closing an investigation, also sage your equipment.

6. **Sea Salt** – I have seen investigators make circles around their vehicles with this. Others just draw a line at the doorway. The theory is that spirits can't pass across the salt.

7. **Grounding** – I probably ground myself a dozen times a day. It helps remove stress and negative emotions from your body and mind. To ground, simply imagine negativity passing through you and into the ground. I use my breathing to help me. With every breath in, I pull in positive energy and then push the negative back out. I do this before ghost hunts, but especially afterwards.

8. **Shielding** – This involves using a visualization exercise where you use your own body's energy to build a protective shield around you. Fill it with white light to repel negativity.

During the Investigation

1. Always be respectful. Provoking and promoting ill will is a very good way to get something angry at you. Not only could you bring harm to yourself, but you could put the rest of your team in harm's way as well.
2. Don't ask the spirits to touch you. Unless you are capable of pushing a spirit off you, don't allow it to get any closer than an arm's length away from you.
3. Don't offer for the spirits to use your energy. This goes back to allowing them into your space. If you aren't capable of pushing them off you, don't invite them close. If they do use your energy, you will find yourself drained for days. It's not worth the risk.
4. Don't go anywhere alone. Always travel in groups of two or more. If one of you were to get injured, by falling, tripping, or any number of things, someone can go for help. Also, if you see or hear something paranormal, it's always good to have a witness.
5. Always close EVP or Spirit Box sessions, telling the spirits they must remain where they are.

After the Investigation

1. Do a closing prayer of your choice. We often recite the St. Michael's prayer again.
2. Burn some sage. This helps cleanse the air and increase the harmony.
3. Grounding is helpful at this time, too.
4. Tell the spirits they cannot follow you. Tell them their feet are firmly grounded where they are.

5. Don't linger at the investigation site. As soon as you've ended the investigation, get moving. You don't want to give anyone a second chance to tag along.

6. When you get home, bathe. Some people shower, but I always prefer to take a bath with a touch of sea salt in it to wash off any residue of the investigation. I also cleanse my protection stones at the same time, and then set them on a window sill to soak up the moonlight.

7. Eat something healthy and then get a good night's sleep. This fortifies you and helps you build your energy back up. Investigations are often very draining. Half the battle for staying protected during an investigation is making sure you're taking good care of yourself. If your energy is high, you'll be far less attractive to spirit attachment. They'd rather go for an easier target, if this is what they're looking for. Keep in mind that many spirits are firmly attached to a location and have no desire to follow you, but it's still important to be careful. The one percent who would like to follow you are looking for an opportunity. Don't give it to them.

8. Hold the faith. Don't doubt what you are doing is effective. If you've read my story, you'll know why.

Keys for a Successful EVP Session

EVP: Electronic Voice Phenomenon.

Following a few basic rules makes the session go much smoother.

1. Be considerate. Once an EVP session begins, sit down and restrict your movements as much as possible. If you are using other equipment, such as a camera or a video recorder that makes noises when in use, restrict the usage and always identify the sounds your equipment makes as it happens. There's nothing more frustrating than being forced to throw something out because of possible noise contamination.

2. Plan your wardrobe with noise reduction in mind. Don't wear anything made of nylon or any other fabric that makes a sound when it moves, such as corduroy. If you wear jewelry, make sure it doesn't clank together when it moves or makes any other noises. Shoes should always have soft soles. Silence is the overall goal. You don't want your clothing speaking for you.

3. Research your location ahead of time so you can ask relevant questions regarding the history or names of people who once lived there. Sometimes this gives you a much better response.

4. Establish ahead of time whether there is going to be a leader or if all participants are going to ask questions.

5. Space your questions out 30 seconds, giving the spirit world a chance to answer. Sometimes it takes them a while to either work up the energy or the courage to speak and you don't want their response to come in the middle of your next question.

6. Mark ambient noises. If a car drives by or if someone sniffles, identify it out loud. You'll be thankful later when you are reviewing the hours of audio. Yawns and stomach growls can

sound just like whispers and growls on tape - mark them. If you have set up in a location with a lot of traffic outside, try moving to another location with less ambient noises or be sure to mark it on your audio that you are in a high traffic location. There's no need to mark every car that goes by, but do mark the especially loud ones.

7. If possible, record the session on video as well. This will give you the opportunity to rule out a possible ambient noise later if you can see all of the participants.

8. Use multiple voice recorders. Sometimes the spirits are selective in the devices they choose to speak on. Their voices will often appear on one recorder, but not another.

9. Identify yourself at the beginning of a session - we often go around the room and just state our names and give a quick greeting. Treat it as if you are a guest in someone's house, because you are.

10. Remember your manners. Provoking might give you more than you bargained for, so be considerate with your questions. Ghosts were (are?) people, too. The ones who weren't people (inhuman, demonic), aren't anything you want to make angry.

11. Limit the amount of people in your session to three or four people. The larger the group, the more chances there will be that someone will sniffle or have a growling stomach. It also can be a bit intimidating to the spirit world, having a massive group all firing questions at them. Would you rather walk into a huge group setting or an intimate group setting?

12. We usually capture most of our good EVPs at the very beginning and the very end of sessions. Always remember to tell them that you are getting ready to end the session to give them one more chance to respond.

13. Keep your sessions relatively short. We've found that after 20 to 30 minutes, we get much less than we do in shorter, 10 to 15 minute sessions. Play around with this and find what

works for you. Try different areas.

14. Do not whisper in an EVP session. Speak in your normal voice. A whisper will sound like an EVP later when you review your tape, and will get your hopes up for no good reason.

15. Do not eat, chew gum loudly, smoke or do anything else that will make a noise on the recorder. If you must take a drink of water, identify it out loud as a tag, so you'll know later when you're reviewing the audio.

16. Determine a session method ahead of time. If you are one of those people who likes to record for a short period of time and then review it immediately, do this in another session or use headphones. Don't ruin someone else's EVP session by contaminating their audio with your frequent playbacks. This goes back to being polite.

17. EVPs can be captured anywhere. Don't limit your sessions to group ghost hunts. Try it everywhere. You'll be surprised at the places where you might get responses.

18. Bring trigger objects. If after doing your research, you learn that the owner of the home once loved gardening, bring along a gardening shovel or a flower. Some researchers will bring music to play prior to the session to lure in spirits.

19. Keep your eyes open as well as your ears. You might catch something.

20. Using external microphones cuts down on the internal noises your recorder makes.

21. If you walk while you record, be prepared to throw out a great deal of possible evidence. You don't realize how much noise you make while walking until you listen to it played back at triple volume.

22. Make sure everyone is on the same page. If one group is chasing shadows and another group is using a Frank's Box or Ovilus, space yourselves out far enough so you can't hear one

another.

23. Have fun with it. Sometimes during our sessions, we have a period where we lighten up and just talk amongst ourselves for a minute or two. This tends to give us good responses afterwards.

The end

Please keep reading for a preview of my latest paranormal true story thriller Bones in the Basement.

Bones in the Basement

Surviving the S.K. Pierce Victorian Mansion

Edwin Gonzalez & Lillian Otero's Story

By

Joni Mayhan

CHAPTER 1

The boy stared up at the creepy old house, feeling a lump grow in his throat.

The other kids wanted to break in and play a game of hide-and-seek. He wasn't sure he wanted to. Something about the house troubled him.

When he drove past it with his mother, he always glanced up at the dark windows, feeling like someone was watching him. Nobody had lived in the house for as long as he could remember, but everybody knew about it. It was the haunted Victorian mansion.

He went to school with a girl who used to live next door. She talked about seeing faces at the windows and lights blinking off and on all during the night. She told him that a man once burned to death in the house when he spontaneously combusted, and how his ghost still roamed the shadowed hallways. At the time, he swore he'd never go inside that scary old house, but here he was, all the same.

"Are you coming, Trevor?" one of the kids called.

glanced around, noticing that he was the only one who crawled through the basement window yet. He ved the lump in his throat, wanting very badly to retreat afety of his home and watch an episode of *Scooby Doo* instead, but he couldn't figure how to do it without looking like a chicken.

He gave the house one more cautious glance and then climbed in after his friends.

I'll only stay for a little while. Then I'll tell them I have to go home for something.

They crept in through a basement window. The space was so dark, all he could see was the bobbing light from the flashlight ahead of him. Something brushed the back of his neck and he jolted with a gasp.

The other kids jumped too, but soon laughed as they realized what happened.

"What's the matter, Trevor? Afraid of a little spider's web?"

He took a deep breath to steady his nerves and tried to shake off the feeling that wouldn't leave him. They weren't supposed to be there. He could feel it in every cell of his body.

At the top of the stairs they found a doorway that led to the first floor. Trevor looked around, taking in the wooden floors and the furniture covered by sheets. It was exactly what he thought of when he imagined a haunted house. The only thing missing was the ghosts.

As they tiptoed through the old house, they began hearing strange sounds. At first, the sounds were subtle. They heard the creak of a floorboard in another room, which was followed by the echo of footsteps on the grand staircase.

One of the children started counting, so he scrambled up the grand staircase to the second floor to look for a hiding place.

The first room he came to had red walls. Something about the room made him feel uncomfortable, as if someone hid in the corner watching him. He gave the doorway a wide berth and studied the second room he came to.

It looked like it could have been a kid's bedroom. It was small and square, with two doorways and a strange looking closet. Something about the closet appealed to him. The door was short, as if it was made for a kid. As he stood in front of it, he heard the counting girl reach twenty.

"Ready or not, here I come," she announced.

He opened the closet door and scrambled in.

The darkness nearly closed in on him, so he cracked the door an inch and allowed a ribbon of light inside. He watched several kids run past the doorway, looking for a place to hide, as the counter made her way up the stairs.

"I see you, Jimmy!" she yelled.

Trevor held his breath, praying she didn't look in his direction. If she did, she'd probably find him in a second. It wasn't exactly the greatest hiding spot.

She continued past, and he let out his breath.

I made it.

He listened as the girl walked up the narrow staircase to the third floor, thinking that he'd just stay in the closet until all the other children were found. He heard the sound of more footsteps in the hallway. As he leaned forward to see who it was, something happened that would haunt him for the rest of his life. Hands grabbed onto his shoulders.

"Get out!" a voice whispered in his ear, before giving him a shove forward.

He stumbled out of the closet, a scream lodged deep in his

throat.

As he rounded the doorway, he turned back in time to see a transparent boy grinning at him from the depths of the closet he'd just departed. He didn't stop running until he reached his own doorstep.

He wouldn't return to the house until years later, until his aunt Marion took him on a tour.

Edwin Gonzalez and Lillian Otero when they first met

CHAPTER 2

Edwin's stomach twisted into knots as they drove to look at a Victorian mansion in Gardner. He wasn't sure why they were driving so far to look at a house. They already had a house, and he was perfectly happy where they were, but once Lillian caught wind of the mansion, there was no resisting her. Lillian loved Victorians like some women loved fine jewelry.

He glanced at her sitting in the passenger seat, her long black hair pulled into a high, sleek ponytail. She wore heavy silver earrings that swung back and forth as her head bobbed to the beat of the music. Her happiness was nearly contagious. He couldn't help smiling at her, causing some of his uneasiness to slough away.

It was hard to believe they'd been together for over twenty years. They met at the bindery factory where they both worked at the time. He was blown away the first time he saw her walking across the parking lot, her dark hair dancing around her face as she laughed. He was enamored in an instant, something he still felt years later. There was nothing he wouldn't do for her.

Their happily-ever-after led them to an ordinary existence in Dorchester, a Boston neighborhood, where they shared a triple-decker with Lillian's mother and sister. Life was comfortable, if not predictable, with the fixtures of friends and family surrounding them like a safety net. The days passed by with a steady hum, the highs and lows too minimal to notice. Days were spent working at their respective jobs, while weekends were consumed by daytrips to antique stores and to local restaurants, or doing repairs around the house. Everything changed when Lillian's sister showed her a real estate listing for a Victorian mansion. Their lives were promptly fractured into a thousand pieces. Nothing would ever be comfortable or predictable again.

Edwin wasn't sure what to make of Lillian's sudden need to see the house.

It was more than just a passing fancy or a decision made after seeing something alluring and wanting a closer look. It was more of an obsession, a dire need as magnetic as the pull of addiction. Once she saw the listing, she had to go there. There was no other option.

It troubled Edwin on several levels. Lillian was usually so fastidious. She wasn't reckless or prone to impulse. She had an agenda, and she usually stuck with it. It was one of the things he loved most about her. She was consistent. She made lists and schedules; she thought things out to the last detail before she reacted. He knew what to expect of her, and it gave him a great sense of comfort. Her suggesting they go look at a house sixty miles out of town was very much out of character for her. At first, he blamed it on her passion for Victorians.

Lillian had loved Victorians since she was a little girl. She used to live down the street from a beautiful Victorian. She walked past it every day on her way to school, swearing that one day she'd have a house just like it. The dream stayed with her through her adulthood. He often caught her scrolling through the real estate listings, daydreaming about owning one, but it had never advanced to a point where they actually got in the car to go look at one.

By the way she described it, the house they were driving to sounded similar to the house of her childhood dreams. The Second Empire Victorian mansion was over six-thousand square feet in size, and had twenty-six rooms, including a tower that rose above the house, providing sweeping views of South Gardner. According to the realtor, the house had been vacant for the past two years as the owner tried to find a buyer. Every deal that came through for the house mysteriously fell apart. It was as if the house was waiting for the right owner.

"Are you excited?" Edwin asked, reaching over to hold Lillian's hand.

She turned, her lips curving into a broad smile that lit up her entire face. "I'm beyond excited. Just imagine living in our own Victorian," she said, staring wistfully off into space.

Edwin wished he could be half as excited.

Part of his anxiety was based in reality. Victorians were known to be money pits. An old house would require a lot of upkeep, something he wasn't sure they could handle both physically and financially. He imagined the long hours and the added expenses, and it was enough to make him sigh. The other reason was the uneasy feeling in his gut.

Something just wasn't right about that house.

He knew it from the minute he called the realtor to request a viewing. The woman had been very strange about it. She asked him at least three times if he was sure he wanted to see *that* house.

And then there was the dream.

He'd barely fallen asleep the night before, when he found himself in the middle of the strangest dream.

In the dream, he found himself drifting through the massive front door of a Victorian mansion. It was as though he didn't have feet or legs. He just floated along like a ghost on the wind. He looked up to see a bright chandelier shining above him, the light casting dark whimsical shadows into the corners of the room. To his right, he heard the melodic sound of music.

It was soft and enchanting, the kind of music people listened to at the turn of the century. The house had a glorious feeling to it, as if people were at the highest peak of their lives, thoroughly enjoying all the wealth and splendor it offered them. It was like a vintage snapshot in time, encapsulating the souls who refused to relinquish the moment. He felt himself traveling towards a set of white doors towards the source of the music, unable and unwilling to stop.

The doors swung open as he approached them, and he found

himself in the midst of a large social gathering.

People crowded inside the parlor room, dressed in early Victorian finery. Ice cubes clinked in glasses as drinks were served, and the hum of conversation filled the air. Women with bright smiles talked to one another, while dapper men shared confidences over a glass of finely-aged brandy. The room smelled of perfume and pipe smoke, which caught the light as it clouded the air.

No one seemed to notice him as he silently wafted into the room.

He floated among them as if he were invisible.

They smiled and talked to one another, their voices momentarily rising above the lilting sound of the music. As Edwin glided further into the depths, the crowd parted and he became aware of a man sitting in the middle of the room.

Unlike the others, the man was watching him. He was dressed all in black with a debonair mustache that curled upwards at the ends. With his straight carriage and direct gaze, he presented himself as the master of the house. He nodded at Edwin as if welcoming him to the party, a slight knowing smile curving the corners of his lips. And with that, Edwin woke up, feeling disoriented like he just time traveled back from a bygone era.

Lillian squeezed his hand and he glanced back at her, coming back to reality from his daydream. She was still smiling.

"We really need something good to happen to us," she told him.

He sighed again.

It was true. Their dog Casper passed away several months ago, and it was a devastating blow for both of them. Their dogs were like family members, and losing one left a large hole in their lives. Edwin hadn't seen Lillian smile so broadly since

Casper's death. Maybe this would be a good thing for them both.

He tried to clear his mind of the nagging feelings so he could enjoy the moment.

Lillian was right. They needed something good to happen to them.

CHAPTER 3

Bill Wallace sat across the street from the Victorian, nursing a beer at the South Gardner Hotel. Voices and music buzzed around him, but he hardly noticed. His eyes trained through the milky window as he stared at the golden-yellow mansion on the corner.

Something was changing in that house, and he didn't like it.

Bill looked like a cross between Santa Claus and Albert Einstein. With his full white beard and wild hair, he came across as an eccentric sort at first, but there was an intelligence and warmth in his eyes that made people reconsider their first impression.

He always knew he was different. Routine things didn't interest him. He always found himself drawn to the peculiar side of life, the intricacies and the elements that most people never considered. Life was more than what it seemed. He knew this on an empathic, psychic level. While he never called himself a psychic medium, his talents as an empathic medium were undeniable.

His family was known to have the gift of psychic insight. His father used to spend countless hours trying to surprise Bill's grandmother with a visit, but no matter when they showed up at her house, she was ready for them, often with a meal on the table. Bill's own abilities didn't surface until after he died during triple bypass surgery and was successfully resuscitated. When he woke up, he wasn't the same person.

He could talk to ghosts.

Bill could feel the spirits calling to him as he walked the streets of Gardner. He would look up at the side of the buildings, sometimes seeing an apparition standing there, silently watching him. The Victorian Mansion had been pulling at him for several years.

When most people drove past the house, they looked up at the dark windows and wondered if someone was looking back at them. Bill didn't have to wonder. He knew they were there.

The spirit of a young woman named Mattie had been there

since the late 1800's. Petite, with long dark hair that she wore in a bun, she once cared for the Pierce children. Bill saw her as a kind person with a charitable heart, but not someone who tolerated nonsense. Chores were scheduled at specific times, and the children were taught to behave. Even though she was long dead, she remained the protector of the house, keeping it safe from trespassers and ensuring the other resident ghosts behaved themselves.

He became aware of her as he drove past the house on Union Street. He heard the sounds of her in his head, singing a folk song he had never heard before. At the time, he discounted the sound as a consequence from his near-death experience, but after a while he couldn't deny it. She was reaching out to him.

She was calling to him again as he sat across the street, asking for his help.

Unfortunately, Bill had no way of getting inside the house. It had been vacant for two years since the previous owners left. Breaking and entering wasn't something he was willing to do.

"Sorry, Mattie. No can do," he whispered under his breath.

He looked at the house, wondering what was transpiring behind those dark and dingy windows. Whatever it was, it wasn't good.

Bill's relationship with the mansion started in 2000.

He and his friend Mike were sitting on the hood of his car at the pizza shop across the street, waiting for their order. It was late August and the night was thick with humidity and mosquitoes. Mike was talking about the religious training he was undergoing to become a minister, but Bill hardly heard a word he said. All he could do was stare at the house across the street.

He could feel Mattie lingering near a second floor window,

watching him.

Bill was pulled from his daydream when a man burst out of the Victorian mansion and started walking towards them. Bill was immediately captivated by the sight.

The tall, dark-haired man was dressed in a long black coat and had a decided air of confidence to him. Bill laughed when he saw him because, for all the world, he reminded him of Gomez Addams walking out of his creepy haunted house. He was surprised when the man crossed the street and headed towards the pizza shop.

The minute the man approached them, the two made eye contact. Bill, being the jovial type, began humming the theme song to *The Addams Family*. The man seemed taken back for a moment, but recovered after a minute. The two then introduced themselves.

"Mark Veau," the man said, giving Bill a firm handshake. Bill nodded and introduced himself as well, finding himself instantly drawn to Mark's unique character. The fact that he owned such a magnificent house only added to the allure.

"That's a beautiful house," Bill told him, looking over Mark's shoulder at the yellow mansion. It was as though he couldn't look away for long before his gaze was pulled back to those spellbinding windows.

"Would you like to see it?" Mark asked.

Bill nearly lunged for the door. "Very much so," he said, almost forgetting about his friend in his eagerness to see the house.

They came through the door, and Bill felt the outside world melt away. All he could think about was getting upstairs to see Mattie. Mark introduced him to his fiancée Suzanne, but he barely noticed. His gaze was pulled to the staircase.

As they passed the wall to his right, Bill felt a sizzle run up the side of his body. He stopped and looked at his arm. Every hair was standing on end. It was as if the house had an electrical current running right through it. He could feel it buzzing in the air like a pulse.

He found himself walking towards the stairs. He knew it was odd, not waiting for Mark to lead the tour, but there was something about the upstairs that he had to see. It was where Mattie waited. Being so deliciously close was more than he could handle. He needed to see her now.

Even though he never saw the inside the house before, he instinctively knew the layout. He walked up the servant's staircase to the second floor, then made his way down the long hallway.

The space was different than it was in the 1880's when Mattie lived there. The walk-in closet off the master bedroom was once a small sewing room. She liked to sit here and crochet doilies out of bits of string that she found on packages.

The doorway that once connected the room to the second floor landing had been plastered over many years ago, turning it into a closet. Mattie still spent ample amounts of time there, preferring the quietness of the room to the more congested areas of the house. It was where she went to collect her thoughts.

Mattie.

The minute she noticed him, she reached out to him with her mind. She seemed happy to see him, pleased to finally find someone who could communicate with her. She told him many things, the words nearly tumbling out too fast for comprehension. It was as though she'd kept them bottled up for decades and the pressure of releasing them was just too much for her to handle.

"Bill?" Mark said, touching his arm. "Are you okay?"

Bill snapped out of it long enough to explain. "Every time I drive by, she calls to me. She likes it here," he said.

Mark gave him a curious glance. "Are you talking about Mattie Cornwell? The nanny?" he asked.

Bill was surprised that Mark knew about Mattie. "You know about her?"

Mark smiled. "Several weeks after we moved in, our contractor told us the house was haunted and asked if he could bring in his two nieces who were mediums. They told me about her," he said with an incredulous tone. "How do you know about her?"

Bill told Mark about his gift, never worrying that the other man would think he was crazy. There seemed to be an instant understanding between the two of them that the friendship would never be what other people considered normal. Bill was just as colorful as Mark.

"She takes care of the house. She always has," he told Mark. "This house sat empty for over twenty years before you bought it. Do you ever wonder how this house made it through the years of being abandoned without suffering immense damage?" he asked.

Mark looked at him inquisitively. "What do you mean?"

Bill pointed to the pristine woodwork that framed every window, doorway, floor, and ceiling. "You would think after twenty years of sitting empty with people sneaking in here day and night, someone would have carved their initials into the woodwork, or even burned one of the doors for warmth. Mattie's the reason why they didn't."

Mark nodded and then shared a story of his own. "I've had several psychics tell me the same thing. There's even a police report to prove it. Back in the seventies, Mattie chased two guys out of here," Mark said.

"Really?"

Mark smiled. "Yeah, they were just thugs. They were were up to no good. They broke into the house, thinking they were going to steal something, but they got the crap scared out of them instead. Somebody called the police because one of the guys ended up outside on the ground in a fetal position blubbering about being chased out of the house. Apparently, the cops searched the house and didn't find anyone inside. They told the guy on the sidewalk that he must have imagined it. There was nobody in the house. The guy looked up at them from the sidewalk and stated, 'I said we were chased out of the house. I didn't say it was somebody,'" Mark finished with a smile.

He went on to share what he knew about Mattie Cornwell.

She was born in 1859 in Nova Scotia, Canada. She was twenty-one when she came to work for the Pierce family as a servant in the house. Her primary focus was caring for the Pierce children. She was firm but loving with the children, keeping them mindful of their manners and helping them grow into the influential men they would one day become.

Later research would show that Mattie died at the young age of twenty-five from an acute inflammation of the hip just two years after getting married. Her tragedy would be just one among many at the Victorian mansion. It was as if the house collected them, like some people collected old coins.

Bill opened his mouth to respond, but was suddenly overwhelmed by a tightening in his chest. He slumped back against the wall as the world faded around the edges.

"Are you okay?" Mark asked with concern. "Do you need me to call an ambulance?"

Bill took a few breaths before he answered. Although he felt weak, he was fairly certain he wasn't having another heart attack. It was something else altogether. It was the house. It was getting to him. "No. I'm fine," he finally managed to say. "Just let me catch my breath for a second."

After a few minutes, he began to feel better, but the sensation was momentary. Visions began to flood his mind. He could barely get the words out.

"Mattie doesn't like your dog," he told Mark. "They had dogs at the mansion, but they were never allowed to run loose around the house. It bothers her because the master of the house would have never allowed it."

Mark seemed taken back. "How do you know I have a dog?" he asked.

Bill stared down at the floor. "Because I can see him in the basement. He's a big black fluffy dog," he said. It was as though he could see straight through the floors.

Mark gave him a dubious look. "That's unreal," he said. "You can really see that?"

Bill wasn't finished with his visions. "There's something in the house that Mattie doesn't like. You need to find it and get it out," he said.

He began to describe an area of the basement, an area he had never seen. "It's in a room with a fieldstone foundation near a set of stairs. It's flat. It might be a document, or a piece of paper, but you'll know it when you see it."

After Bill left, Mark and his wife searched the basement until they found the item Bill had described. It was a canning jar with Nazi swastikas drawn on the label. It was tucked into a bookcase along the backside of the wall behind the servant's staircase. The moment Mark moved the jar across the threshold of the property, a sudden gust of wind caught the label and whisked it away. They never found out who drew the swastikas on the label or why Mattie was so offended by them, but it seemed to appease her nonetheless.

Unfortunately, Mark and Suzanne's marriage only lasted until 2006. When they divorced, the house went back on the market. It took two years before they accepted a solid bid, years that left Bill on the outside looking in again.

Something in the house was changing.

A plan was set into motion and nothing would stop it until it reached the end.

Bones in the Basement is available on Amazon.com in ebook or paperback versions. Click the link below for more information or to download it. Contains EVP links and interviews with paranormal experts. Forward by Thomas D'Agastino.

http://www.amazon.com/Bones-Basement-Surviving-Victorian-Gonzalez-ebook/dp/B00KQQRH72/ref=sr_1_1?ie=UTF8&qid=140309879 2&sr=8-1&keywords=bones+in+the+basement

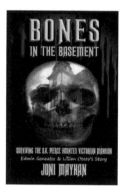 

Note from the author: if you enjoyed the book, please help me better promote it by leaving a positive review on Amazon.com.

Those of us who self-publish truly need your help to find our way to our dreams.

For information about my future writing projects, please check out my website: Jonimayhan.com.

53875781R00098

Made in the USA
Lexington, KY
23 July 2016